DIRTY ENLIGHTENMENT

DIRTY ENLIGHTENMENT:

THE INHERENT PERFECTION OF IMPERFECTION

Peter Brown

The Open Doorway
2007

ISBN-13: 978-1484134849
ISBN-10: 1484134842

CONTENTS

THE INHERENT PERFECTION OF IMPERFECTION

This book is an exploration of our situation.

Most people, if they even care, labor under the mistaken notion that "enlightenment" has something to do with what we DO in our lives; cleaning up our behavior, ratcheting up our compassion, clearing up our obscurations, purifying our bad karma, thinking positive thoughts, thinking NO thoughts, helping little old ladies across the street; in general trying to emulate what we imagine an "enlightened being" acts like - as if the behavior makes the condition.

That's ALL hogwash. It turns out that "enlightenment" is the inherent condition of Being itself. So it's already a done deal. Nothing IN being needs to be cleaned up, purified, made more positive, made more compassionate. The mediocre, imperfect victim most of us fear ourselves to be is already God, without needing to lift a finger! Our world as it is is Heaven, our life already a pageant of Divine Celebration. Hallelujah!

The very fact that any particular condition in our experience even EXISTS at ALL, means it has already crossed the finish line. Being equals enlightenment. Period. If any condition IS, it is inherently absolutely perfect. The clouds in the sky, the shit in the toilet. Tag, YOU'RE IT. You may as well sell your mala and trade in your meditation robe for a bikini and go work on your tan, it won't make the tiniest bit of difference to the ACTUAL condition of anyone or anything whether or not you do.

You'd think that fact would put a lot of people in the "spirituality" industry out of business, wouldn't you? But I'm afraid they don't have to worry, and can probably go on selling water to the fish for the foreseeable future. The unfortunate fact, at least for those of us pushing for the dissemination of this truth, is that people are pretty damn absorbed in their dramatic struggle to find what they haven't lost, and are pretty likely to go on muddling along the "path to being" and the "journey to now" like tired horses with blinders on, even though they ARE, and exactly WHEN does it happen to be?

This book goes into this fact at great length, from many points of view. It's a bit of a smorgasbord, with several parts, incorporating discussions, pedantic explanations, aphorisms, anecdotes; really pretty much something for everyone. So please, if you find yourself interested in what really IS, AS IT IS, and what that means to "you", explore its pages to your heart's content... and you just might even "get it"!

OUR SITUATION

Reality is indescribable; yet we each know it intimately, never having known anything else whatsoever.

But we might not KNOW that we know it. We commonly mistake our conceptual misinterpretations and oversimplified understandings of what reality is, arrived at through our programming and early assumptions, to be true. We thereby become blinded to the obvious fact of the way reality is already ACTUALLY functioning in, and as, our experience RIGHT HERE, RIGHT NOW.

Our only impediment to true self-knowledge is our inaccurate beliefs about what we are and what the world is, which we mistakenly hold to be true. The solution to this impediment is to examine the ACTUALITY of our experience, and using discrimination, logic, and direct seeing, understand for ourselves the inaccuracies of our previously-held modeling of our situation, and let go of erroneous beliefs about "the world". This is really a very simple process; it is only WE that can complicate it.

We each have accumulated a complex story about what we are and what our lives are, that incorporate many assumptions and conclusions that were arrived at when we were immature and did not have the discriminative capacities to critically examine them. These assumptions may have been learned from the teaching or example of those we perceived around us, our families and immediate culture; and we accepted them as truth, and incorporated them into the edifice of our belief system, using them as the basis for further ideas about ourselves and our situation.

We have tended to be seduced by the emotional investment that arises from some beliefs we may have arrived at; for example "I am separate from the universe", "I am vulnerable and potentially in danger", "I am needy and might not be able to get what I need", and so on. Building on these and similar basic beliefs and their elaborations, most of us concoct an elaborate soap opera with ourselves as the star, full of imaginary hopes and fears, dangers and rewards, energized by self-importance and heightened emotionality.

Thus most of us find ourselves living in a fantasy, a dream-world, ignoring any actual experience that doesn't fit in with our oversimplified and self-referential beliefs; we are sleepwalkers.

So what can we do to "wake up" from this internally consistent dream of self-importance based on fantasies?

The fortunate truth is that we ALL have intimate access to Reality; in fact we have never experienced anything ELSE, and ARE nothing but Reality ourselves, inherently. So all we need to do is take stock of the actuality of our situation.

The rub is that to do this, we have to be able and willing to at least partially suspend our belief in our accumulated "story", in order to see through it, to perceive the actual facts of our experience. Once we have done this once, it can be easier to follow through with further investigation of the truth of our situation; but we ultimately need luck (good OR bad!) to motivate that first peek out from under the numbing blanket of our concepts.

So generally only people who have already become somewhat disenchanted with their story have any interest in this investigation (with the exception of those many people who try to use the investigation, "being spiritual", as an element IN their story, for status or prestige, etc.).

This book is for YOU. If you are looking at it, you are probably at least starting to be ready for it, beginning to open to the possibility of a "real life" beyond your pretenses, or perhaps are already in the midst of fighting your way out of your cocoon, ready to be born in TRUTH.

AWAKENING

I was 22 years old in the summer of 1973, living in Miami. I was a rock musician, living a typical ex-hippie lifestyle, I suppose. Late nights, late mornings, lots of young friends and parties; pretty hedonistic.

But I was an oddball, an ugly duckling; as long as I could remember as a child, I KNEW that there was "more going on than meets the eye". There HAD to be; life didn't make any sense, and I reasoned that this "X-factor" would make everything fit into place, explain everything.

At first, I thought that everybody, all the adults, were in on it and knew what it was, and I just didn't get it because I was a small child; and that as I grew I would begin to fathom it and grow into this certain knowledge, maybe be "initiated" into it when I reached a certain age. But of course as I grew, the world and the many human explanations for it that I encountered seemed to make less and LESS sense, and I began to have the horrifying suspicion that despite my expectations, maybe all these "adults" didn't have any more of a clue than I did as to what was "going on", maybe even LESS of one.

I began a steady search on my own, for some traces of the meaning of it all, this "X-factor" that would make everything fit together. At first, as an older child, I was drawn to archaeology and ancient history, archeo-sociology, astronomy, and superficial overviews of the various sciences and comparative religion. Then in my middle and later teens, I discovered the fascinating fact that there were "secret" traditions that claimed to have an "inside track" on things, and I began a voracious study of occultism; quabalah, tarot, the "witch" traditions, ritual magic, yoga, and much more. At the same time more conventionally I was fascinated by the then-burgeoning study called parapsychology.

I had made the acquaintance of a friend of my mother's named Pino Turolla during my early teen years. He was an Italian count living in Miami with his wife and soon-to-be son, a friendly if slightly peculiar man, and for the first few years that I knew of him he meant nothing special to me, just another of the many friends of my mother and stepfather. Eventually I discovered that he was an archaeologist of sorts, who spent much of his time adventuring in South America searching in the amazon for the remnants of ancient civilizations. When I discovered this, he became a very much more interesting figure to me because of my interest in archaeology and primitive people's world views.

So I arranged through my mother to visit him at his home in Miami Beach. He was very gracious that first visit, showing off his mind-boggling collection of pre-Columbian artifacts that he had recovered from the jungles of Ecuador; we seemed to hit it off. He intimated intriguing and perhaps eccentric theories about the world views and magical traditions of the ancient peoples who had produced these artifacts, that piqued my interest in this man even more, as I was beginning my own interest in these "occult" areas of human experience.

Over time a friendship formed, and he took me under his wing, allowing me to visit more and more frequently, sharing time in relaxed discussion. He had an apparently endless supply of stories of his adventures among the Ecuadorian Indians, with the exploits of their "brujos", medicine men and social leaders, featuring prominently. I quickly became aware that he had experienced mysterious interactions with these apparently powerful people that he claimed had changed him forever, making him "psychic".

Needless to say, all this was right up my alley, and I ate it up. I was fascinated to speculate that maybe I had actually met someone who had direct involvement with these mysterious aspects of human experience that I had placed my hopes for life's answers into.

But I was also a bit intimidated. He was "larger than life" to me, a powerful man in his fifties who had the courage to single-handedly pursue these amazing investigations among people so foreign to the culture that I knew, while at the time I was an insecure teenager. Temperamentally he was not inclined to be a teacher per se, but seemed at ease sharing his experience in his own way as stories; and I took a passive role and waited for him to get around to those areas of his experience that most interested me in his own time.

During these occasional visits over the next several years I learned that he had had a life threatening experience quite a few years previously in the amazon jungle, being severely bitten by a piranha-like fish while scuba prospecting for diamonds in a river many days from civilization. This was before his interests had turned to archaeology. It turned out that one of the Indian guides that were assisting him in his prospecting was a brujo, much respected within his people. Using a poultice made with local herbs that he sent his compatriots out to retrieve from the jungle, in addition to laying on of hands and chanting, this man treated Pino's wounds. They then carried him for a day to the airfield that had been hacked out of the rainforest, where he would be picked up as scheduled in a few days time, there being no way to contact the pilot from the jungle. The medicine man then mixed up a potion of "medicine", which he told Pino to drink whenever he felt hungry or thirsty. Then he and his fellows left, leaving Pino in the small hut by the landing strip with the medicine.

Pino subsequently found out that the "medicine" that the brujo left for him was a type of ayahuasca, a very powerful mind-altering drug. Pino dutifully drank the potion, and said he had amazing visions where all the animals of the rainforest visited him and shared their visionary powers with him.

After a few days the plane arrived, got Pino down to Quito and on a plane to Miami. His leg was still bandaged in its poultice, and being a modern, civilized man, having been treated with such primitive medical practices (which included several of the men urinating on the poultice), he fully expected that when he got to Miami he would have to have his leg amputated for gangrene. He called his wife René from the Quito airport telling her which flight he would be on, and to arrange with the hospital for treatment when he arrived.

They went directly to the hospital from the airport; and when the doctor first removed the poultice, he asked, "WHEN did you say this bite happened? It looks almost completely healed".

Pino related how this shook his world view, forcing a much deeper respect for the magical approach of the Indians to life. But then, after several days home, he woke up sitting naked out on his back lawn in lotus posture, having had visions in his dreams. He thought he was going crazy.

From then on his life opened into newness. He related how he received teachings in his dreams, which he called "night school", had visions, and seemed to have access to information directly in his mind from no known source. The model through which he tried to understand what was happening to him was parapsychology, which at the time was a newly-emerging study on the fringes of physics. He was himself eventually studied for his abilities at the Stanford Research Institute.

I moved away from Miami in 1968 at the age of 17, and saw Pino very infrequently over the next several years. During this time I pursued my obsessive studies in search of the key that would explain the world and my life. I studied Rosicrucianism, alchemy, spiritualism, modern western initiatory magic, and expanded my search into the lives of eastern saints and the practices of raja yoga, jnana yoga, and bhakti yoga.

Then in 1972 at the age of 21 I returned to Miami, and was able to see Pino much more frequently. His life had been developing amazingly; he was a respected healer, still pursued his interests in South America, and had become integrated into the "psychic underground" of the time. This was pre- "new age" times, and these people were both more respected than they might be now, for being involved in the then-more mainstream scientific parapsychology studies, and simultaneously more on the fringes of what was widely acceptable by society. He was acquainted and intimate with many of the prime figures in the "psychic" world at the time, and his own abilities had grown. He told me of an occasion when he and his family were at a restaurant, when all the silverware at their table started bending spontaneously ala Uri Geller; he said they covered the silverware with their napkins and hurried out of the place before they were blamed for the damage.

Then one day in 1973 came the most surprising day of my life. I woke up one morning with a very strange experience occurring in my field of awareness. I felt as if the top of my head had opened; there was a huge, open presence at the top portion of my awareness, which seemed to be very intelligent and seemed to be communicating with me on a non-verbal level. It was unlike anything I had experienced previously, and I had no clue what was going on. This was not an idea or a displaced physical sensation, it was a self-validating presence the like of which I had never experienced. I thought I was being visited by angels or something.

I immediately realized that Pino would be the only person I knew or knew of who might possibly have any idea what was happening to me, so I phoned him up, and he invited me to come right over. I told him what I was experiencing as best I could. He then started talking to me much more intimately than he ever had, about what we are and what our experience is. As he talked, I followed the words he used, and simultaneously felt the nature of this new openness in my experience and the obvious state from which he was clearly speaking, and I could see that they were one. I could see with certainty that he KNEW what he was, and he KNEW what I was, and seeing THAT enabled ME to see what I was. There was absolute clarity and certainty in the understanding that arose in me, that I saw was shared precisely with the understanding that Pino held. Our communication immediately went to a depth I had never before experienced; the words we were exchanging reflected a shared direct experiencing of energy-states in real-time, and I understood for the first time what it means to be "psychic", and saw the truth of Pino's state, and saw that it was actually also my own state.

I clearly saw, concurred with by Pino verbally and nonverbally, that I was actually a disembodied Intelligence within which what I called "the world" appeared, and that the energy of that experiencing was one with my being. I was astounded. I can't possibly communicate the depth of my surprise at this revelation, and the obvious certainty that it included. I saw that I am a vast intelligence, and that I owned whatever energy of experience appeared within me; and even as Pino appeared in my world and I in his, in actuality we were each the sovereign and the sole inhabitant in our own universe. The entire "material" universe that I thought I had been living in all along dissolved completely, and I saw the unassailable truth of this new perspective.

And perhaps the most surprising revelation was that I saw that I had ALWAYS been what I was now newly seeing myself to be, I just hadn't seen it as it is clearly. Astounding! HOW had I not noticed this amazing but wholly obvious state of affairs?

That was the turning point in my life, my second birth. But it turned out I had a long second adolescence ahead of me.

Pino pushed me away within a few months after that day. We had a falling out over his opinion of my girlfriend at the time, eventually to become my wife; but I since came to realize that he was "kicking me out of the nest", trying to force me to become more self-reliant. I retained the essential perspective of that revelation I had had, but over the next twenty four years, found myself struggling with the realities of my life. Somehow I couldn't seem to reconcile that perspective with the details of being the fallible, struggling human being I manifestly was appearing as. I was distant from Pino, both physically and egoically, so didn't have much more opportunity to try to work through this with him; then suddenly he died in 1984, of a massive heart attack.

I searched for another person who had the obvious REAL experience of the truth of our state to work with, but found no one. I could see Muktananda knew when I met him, but he was unavailable within the complexities of his organization. Otherwise, all the prospective candidates I encountered were either obviously off the mark, or in reality no "farther along" than I was. No one that I saw was a conscious, full manifestation of the divine as I had been shown Pino had been; so I struggled on alone.

Then in 1996 I was diagnosed with cancer. I was bedridden for four months and incapacitated for another several months, an experience which plunged me deeply to the bedrock of my being, and forced me finally to surrender. As I recovered, I came to realize that the problems I had been grappling with for twenty-four years were based on a very simple belief that I had not resolved even in my experience with Pino. Somehow, I had unconsciously retained the subtle belief that the manifest world of my experience was somehow a separate entity from the overarching intelligence I saw.

But now I was able to see the fallacy of that belief, and it evaporated like the mirage that it was. I saw clearly that BEING IS ONE "THING", and I AM THAT, as indeed is all "else". "I" have rested in that certainty since that day in February, 1997.

Our true situation is indescribable, even as we ARE It and nothing else. This indescribability is one of the facts that perpetuates Its obscurity for people. If It was readily describable, then those that understand It clearly could just describe It to those that don't, removing their confusion. But this is not the case.

The reason It is indescribable is due to Its nature. Our actual situation is infinite, open-ended, inherently subjective (in that there are no fixed, stable objective conditions that can be delineated), indefinable in rational terms, and ungraspable as specific reference points, conditions, or objects, from which one could derive some orientation. Faced with that fact, how to try to communicate It using finite words to those that are confused as to Its actual nature? The description seems as confusing as our misunderstandings of what It is seem, maybe even more so.

And this is the crux of the matter; it is exactly BECAUSE the true nature of our situation is so indefinable that we are motivated to manufacture simplified, understandable, stable, finite, rational models and descriptions of ourselves and our world, to give us a sense (albeit false) of security and safety in the midst of this seeming chaos. Then these manufactured beliefs about our situation become the very thing that most stands in the way of our seeing the true state of affairs as It is.

Although reality as It is is indescribable, It IS directly knowable. In fact, of course, we have never known or experienced anything else whatsoever. How could we? If we experienced something "unreal", what would it be made of? How could it appear to us? If something appears in our experience, it must be made of real "stuff", be substantially and essentially consisting of reality. Of course, the interpretation of what it IS in consciousness might be inaccurate... That is the only way that anything we experience might be said to be "unreal".

REALITY AS EXPERIENCE

Experience can be described as constantly changing, non-repeating unknown energies appearing in consciousness. What these energies consist of, or what causes them to appear, is the fundamental mystery; they spontaneously appear within consciousness, and are inextricably one with consciousness, so the "mechanism" of consciousness and experiences are one and the same. To bother to differentiate the one from the other is arbitrary. They never appear independently from each other.

We commonly (and actually arbitrarily), differentiate experience into different fields on the basis of their relative qualities; then designate the fields as "vision", "touch", "smell", "taste","hearing", and "thought", perhaps including others such as emotion, intuition, "vibes", etc.. (Various theories about "bodies" and "sense organs" are further elaborated based on these common distinctions.)

Within any one of these fields, the flow of energies (apparent "objects") is spontaneously appearing, constantly changing and non-repeating, and instantaneously disappearing as present conditions are changing; yet nevertheless various degrees of patterning to the energy flows can be differentiated, giving rise to ideas of "objects". Yet in Reality the patterning might be said to be like a weather system, where continuously varying conditions throughout the whole system interactively give rise to particular phenomena in particular locations. A cloud doesn't just appear discretely in the sky, but is a constantly changing result of interacting conditions throughout the entire atmosphere; so although it appears to be in one place, it is a manifestation of the whole system nonlocally. Likewise the patterning observable in the "sensory" fields does not really consist of discrete objects, for no particular "object" can exist without, or outside of, the rest of its field of energies; and without that field it would not exist, exactly like the example of a cloud in the sky. For example, the chair I see across the room can't be lifted out of my entire field of vision; when I close and open my eyes, the chair disappears and reappears as one with the field. So although various degrees of patternings can be observed in the sense fields (including "thought"), these patternings do not indicate discrete objects that exist with any degree of independence at all.

Likewise the differentiation of the various sense fields from each other is arbitrary, as they cannot be separated or extricated from each other; but arise as a complex, inextricably unified-in-real-time field of experience. And even differentiating the unified fields of experience from consciousness is likewise equally arbitrary, as the one never appears without the other; so why bother with the designations "one" and "other"...

So we are left with Reality apparently being a wholly mysterious "consciousness/energies field", consisting of nothing but itself; experienced by nothing but itself; and miraculously appearing *in itself* as a unified, infinitely complex, ever-changing, never-repeating open-ended whole, within which infinitely complex degrees of patternings are spontaneously simultaneously appearing/disappearing. This is close to the true picture. Now, commonly people are indoctrinated during their upbringing into a complex set of beliefs about Reality; that might include ideas that they are small, independent, material entities descended from apes, living within a huge, objectively-existing material universe that is separate from them, and consisting of myriad, independent objects interacting chaotically; and that their existence, fulfillment, and persistence, depends upon the achieving or avoiding of certain objectively-existing situations that they have limited power to enact/avoid. This might be the common world view of the majority of humans.

That model is profoundly different from that arrived at by our examination above. We have seen that no discrete objects can be meaningfully differentiated from the field of experience, and that the Experiencer (consciousness) can't be meaningfully differentiated from the objective energies of experience, so on that basis alone, every element of that common model of our situation is refuted.

So... how does it come to be that in the face of our constant, clear experiencing of the reality of our being as it always is, most of us come up with stories about what we are and what our supposed situation is, that diverge so greatly from what it ACTUALLY is?

CONFUSION

The fundamental cause of our problems is that consciousness has the property of being able to fantasize, to hypothesize; in other words, to create imaginary conceptual models in consciousness.

This property in itself is not a problem; BUT, it seems to happen that consciousness can mistake its imaginary models for actuality. That, along with the evanescent and open-ended nature of appearances, (which renders them susceptible to being easily interpreted in a skewed way, according to any conceptual bias with which they are observed), makes it possible that consciousness can lose its clear understanding of itself and its actual functioning, in a maze of imaginary interpretations; stories about "what's happening".

Once this happens, it can be very difficult for consciousness to find its way "back" to a clear perception of what is ACTUALLY happening, unclouded by the imaginary interpretations that have confused it. The erroneous interpretations that consciousness gets muddled in tend to imply further errors in modeling, by the "garbage in, garbage out" principle, thus causing the confusion to proliferate itself. This is apparently the situation for the vast majority of humankind.

Those that want to "awaken", i.e. want to clearly see the reality of their situation as it actually IS, have to first somehow acquire an inkling that their current understandings of their situation might be inaccurate, coupled with a motivation to try to correct that. The impediment to that is the inherent disorientation of being "lost in the dream", and the biggest asset is that: consciousness is, after all, ALWAYS clearly experiencing the reality of its "situation", whether it understands that or not. So even in the midst of confusion, there is a constant immersion of consciousness in reality, the real dynamic energy of experiencing.

The basic element of confusion could be called "entification", belief in the idea that discrete, objectively-existing "entities" exist. Of course in reality nothing actually discrete can be extracted from its milieu, as all aspects of the energy of experience arise, and instantly dissipate, as a continuum in consciousness.

This primary misconception of the supposed existence of entities, opens the door to fantasies of objectively existing environments, worlds, universes; within which myriads of self-existing and discrete entities interact in accordance with various imaginary principles, such as causality and free will. And since such entities can be imagined to both actually exist and to persist, then they might also be vulnerable to destruction...

THUS, the basis for the prime energizer of confusion, FEAR, has been laid.

If consciousness then happens to believe that IT might BE one of these "entities" that it is hypothesizing, and therefore itself might be vulnerable to destruction (death) or partial destruction (pain), the energizing force of FEAR can come into existence. If consciousness strongly identifies itself with a supposed entity (a particular set of sensations as a "body", the formation of EGO), this fear can be a profound motivation to protect the entity (or entities) that are being identified with. This may motivate possible baroque plots and schemes, oriented around extensive manipulation of the supposed OTHER entities that might be threatening the identified-with entities. If such manipulation is anticipated to be not likely of success, then the emotion of despair might be born.

Thus we arrive at the apparent world-view of most of humanity.

(Confusion is also exacerbated by the inherent INFINITY and INDEFINABILITY of the energies which appear in consciousness as experience. Not only does that indefinability readily enable easy misidentification of phenomena as entities, but after the onset of confusion, the obvious indefinability of "things" motivates a redoubled effort to find orientation and stability for ego's safety, through denial and elaboration of the modeling fantasies.)

The fundamental problem with ego's all-consuming defensive schemes, is that the basic elements (entities, identification) of which they are made up, of course DON'T ACTUALLY EXIST in the way they are believed to; so the schemes which are predicated UPON their actual existence, won't ultimately be effective. Therefore frustration, disappointment, and further confusion is the inevitable product of this mechanism.

"Spiritually" speaking, however, this frustration is consciousness's great ALLY, for it serves as the initial motivation for the confused consciousness to investigate whether its fantasies are accurate, opening the door to THE DISCOVERY that they AREN'T, and ultimately to the discovery of the actual nature of reality.

LIBERATION

When consciousness finds itself in clear experiencing, free from erroneous interpretations of that experience, this IS Enlightenment. This is actually the natural, inherent, and continual, condition of consciousness. As this condition seems usually to be arrived at after having been confused previously, then clearly once this clear experiencing is noticed, consciousness can be said to have been "liberated" from the situation of confusion.

This clear experiencing of experience itself is of course consciousness' natural condition, Enlightenment, and paradoxically even the state of confusion turns out on examination to be nothing other than this.

Consider:

Since consciousness ALWAYS experiences nothing whatever other than its own energies arising within itself as experience, then of course confusion is nothing other than this occurring as well. So even in confusion, consciousness is doing nothing whatever other than directly experiencing its own nature functioning, as always. The thinking, fantasizing, conceptual modeling property of consciousness, that enables and generates confusion, is an inherent function of consciousness; as is the ability of consciousness to consider its imaginings to be actual (as of course they are, but ONLY as the energy they ACTUALLY consist of, and NOT as the situations they supposedly present in imagination).

So <u>even in the depths of confusion</u>, nothing whatsoever other than the natural, unadulterated being/functioning of the unique, mysteriously self-existing consciousness is happening, EXACTLY as is the case upon "liberation". This fact enables the "short path" to liberation; to see that that natural condition is already, and always, achieved, by virtue of the inherent inviolable nature of reality. Even CONFUSION is inherently THAT already... what ELSE could it be? SEEING the truth of that total natural functioning of consciousness is liberation, and being caught up in BELIEFS about the "nature of things" is confusion.

REFERENTIAL THOUGHT - the "meaning" of ideas

Another way to describe confusion is the apparent existence of a "second layer" in consciousness. The primary layer is consciousness experiencing its own spontaneously-arising energies directly in itself, as is always and unstoppably happening, which includes the fields of energy that can be classified as "thought". The "second layer" consists of the <u>BELIEF in the objective existence</u> of the conceptual models implied by the functioning of thought-energy in the primary layer.

<u>In other words, the appearance of this "second layer" is created by the belief that thoughts can have real meanings, referring to actual "things".</u>

Of course "thought" is ACTUALLY nothing more than a spontaneously appearing, instantaneously disappearing, unfathomably mysterious energy that appears IN, and is made solely OF, consciousness, as are ALL energies that appear as experience. In actuality it has NO meaning apart from its bare existence, and refers to nothing other than itself, to its being as it is.

This idea that thought is referential, that ideas can represent OTHER ideas or things, is the culprit that enables the seeming existence of this "second layer"; which, once it seems to be appearing in consciousness, tends to become self-perpetuating, as all confusion does. Once the fantasy that ideas can be "about something" takes hold, then ideas about those ideas can proliferate, generating endless apparent complexity to this "second layer".

BUT: There IS no second layer in actuality.

Thought energies appearing in consciousness do NOT refer to anything, or rather refer to everything, as do ALL energies appearing in consciousness; since they are in actuality inextricable from the entire field of energies appearing as experience. This fact CAN be directly seen to be true by consciousness, as there is actually nothing other than the truth of it to be seen. Seeing the inherent falsehood of this "second layer" is another description of the "short path"; and constitutes liberation, since it actually IS nonexistent as a "second" layer: And is in truth nothing other than the spontaneous, miraculous functioning of consciousness, as is everything.

THE PATH

<u>Only the enlightened can truly know what enlightenment actually is.</u>

This fact has enabled the existence of quite a large industry of "spiritual" teachers, books, magazines, and programs, not to mention whole religions and societies, based on the misconception that to find or attain "enlightenment", one needs to change the way one thinks, feels, and/or behaves.

Each of these "paths" proposes various changes that we are supposed to make, in our thinking, feeling, and/or behavior, as well as the means that are supposed to be effective in making those changes; then, supposedly, once we have effectively made those changes, achieved "perfection", we will be enlightened, "spiritually" whole, "illuminated", "liberated", "achieve no-self", united with "God", free of "obscurations", and various other somewhat nebulous-sounding achievements.

We are supposed to variously stop our thinking, generate compassion, achieve equanimity, turn the other cheek, "open" our "heart", calm our energy, "raise" our energy, receive "empowerments", receive energy transfusions of various kinds from people that supposedly have it to give, be humble, dress in certain ways, go through various rigorous programs of behavior involving sitting in certain ways or moving our bodies in certain ways (meditation, prostrations, yoga postures, tai-chi, etc.), not have "negative" emotions, not have "negative" thoughts, and basically surrender our own viewpoint, and do whatever the teacher, program, or religion tells us to do (generally including handing over significant portions of our money). Well, after all, all that sounds like a small(ish) sacrifice to make, if we can gain the prize, achieve the goal, grab that ring as we go spinning by.

And all this plays wonderfully to our habitual self-loathing and self criticism; it makes perfect sense, that OF COURSE! We are deficient, we need to change, improve, be different than we are; THEN everything will be alright, THEN we can live in bliss, THEN we can achieve union with "God". After all, we are "bad", we are weak, we are intimately acquainted with each of our imperfections and flaws, that in our deepest fears we know make us unlovable.

These various "paths" manifestly have a tendency to become self-perpetuating social structures; more interested in recruiting new participants to sustain the organization's structure and those dependent upon it for their raison d'etre, (not to mention sustenance), than upon propagating the goal of personal enlightenment that was the motivation of their original founder.

BUT: What if you already HAVE and ARE the goal you seek? What if there IS no wonderful pot-of-gold-at-the-end-of-the-rainbow that all this elaborate effort is intended to achieve, that isn't ALREADY the case? What if the "problem" isn't that we need to be different than we are, but simply that we don't understand, or notice, what we actually are ALREADY? What if this imperfection that we manifestly include isn't actually imperfection at all?...

THE NON-PATH PATH

As we have seen, even confusion is inherently NOTHING OTHER THAN the natural miraculous functioning of consciousness. This fact means that at ANY time, consciousness can see its true situation, since that is all that is occurring. When this is seen, of course, confusion is short-circuited, and is instantaneously seen to be actually consisting of Enlightenment itself, the natural functioning of consciousness: inherently perfect miraculous energies; appearing within, and made up of, inherently perfect miraculous consciousness.

But HOW does this come about? How can consciousness make the non-leap leap from confusion to clear seeing?

Fortunately, it does it by itself, motivated by its own inherent nature. In fact, until our consciousness internally motivates this leap to seeing, there is absolutely NOTHING that "we" can do to MAKE it happen.

Period.

So, THERE IS NO PATH.

This is not to say that the true process of consciousness starting to notice its actual condition, and struggling to free itself from its own self-generated confusion, might not LOOK an awful lot like our efforts, running around pursuing various peculiar activities with our "bodies, energies, and minds". Reading books, seeking out supposedly useful people to talk with or be in the presence of, sitting, taking drugs, exploring various extreme behaviors; all these activities may be symptoms of consciousness' struggle to awaken from its confusion.

But can "we" DO anything WHATSOEVER that will initiate, or help with, the process?

NO.

Does that mean that we SHOULDN'T pursue all these various activities in the hopes of awakening from confusion? Of course not. It simply means that the TRUE process of awakening does itself, and "we're" just along for the ride. Do these things or not, it will happen when it does, and you won't be ABLE to NOT do what is needed when the time is ripe.

However, you can rest in the comfort that since you find yourself reading this book, it's pretty likely that you are either in the midst of awakening, or soon to be swept into the maelstrom...

I would wish you luck, but you already have all the luck in the universe.

(What we are, what our world is, is impossible to describe in words. It CAN, however, be seen directly, if looked at without any preconceptions. These aphorisms, while not completely true in themselves, are as true as can be stated in words; and may serve as signposts, indicating "where" to look, to SEE for yourself. Read each one one at a time slowly and reflect on it; try to feel or intuit the way in which it might be true. Look directly into your own experience, and see in what way these ideas may indicate the structure of YOUR immediate experience RIGHT NOW, and always...)

Being and consciousness are one and the same. There is no such thing as "objective" being without consciousness; all being is subjective, all being occurs to consciousness.

-Look in your experience and see if this is true-

Consciousness is not a "thing"; it is a capacity to perceive, an openness, a clear field of actuality.

-Look in your experience and see if this is true-

Consciousness has no size, location, or duration. Your awareness does not have a back or sides, top or bottom to it. You can't say how "long it lasts".

-Look in your experience and see if this is true-

Consciousness spontaneously appears in itself alone; it is not contained by, made of, or existing in the space of, anything but itself. Nothing can be found outside of it.

-Look in your experience and see if this is true-

Consciousness is inseparably one with any experience it has. There is zero distance between any experience and the "perceiver". When consciousness experiences "something", it IS that "something".

-Look in your experience and see if this is true-

Consciousness always perceives with perfect clarity and unmediated directness, regardless of what is being perceived.

-Look in your experience and see if this is true-

Consciousness is always exactly the same, regardless of what it is, or isn't, experiencing.

-Look in your experience and see if this is true-

All experience exists within, and is made of, consciousness.

-Look in your experience and see if this is true-

There is nothing but consciousness.

-Look in your experience and see if this is true-

There is no "I" but consciousness; consciousness itself is the only one home.

-Look in your experience and see if this is true-

I AM nothing whatever other than consciousness.

-Look in your experience and see if this is true-

All experience spontaneously appears within consciousness, and never stabilizes or solidifies; it is

always constantly changing, never repeating what it has appeared to be already.

-Look in your experience and see if this is true-

Although experience appears infinitely diversified, not appearing identical with itself at any two places or times, no object can be separated out from the field of experience; and no two objects can be differentiated from each other, except as the inherent differentiation of the field of consciousness within itself.

-Look in your experience and see if this is true-

The entire "material" universe exists within consciousness.

-Look in your experience and see if this is true-

"Thoughts" and "sense objects" are indistinguishable as experiences of consciousness.

-Look in your experience and see if this is true-

"Self" and "other" are arbitrary differentiations, referring to consciousness itself alone.

-Look in your experience and see if this is true-

Consciousness is omnipresent and omniscient. It is always here, and it is what knows, experiences, everything.

-Look in your experience and see if this is true-

It cannot be definitively known what "anything" is except as an experience of consciousness.

-Look in your experience and see if this is true-

"Objects of experience" appear spontaneously within consciousness because of its own inherent nature, as a dream appears spontaneously in the dreaming consciousness because of its inherently creative nature.

-Look in your experience and see if this is true-

Consciousness is the absolute mystery; what it actually is cannot be known; it is the Absolute existing in itself.

-Look in your experience and see if this is true-

There is no consciousness.

-Look in your experience and see if this is true-

DISCUSSION

These are public discussions which took place over the course of a year.

They have been grouped VERY loosely into topics, but there is considerable overlap of subjects addressed, due to the inherently inclusive nature of the fundamental topic; REALITY ITSELF.

EXPERIENCE

-I understand that there's actually only this one perfect, radiant, beingness everywhere, and yet I still seem to see separate people, with their own separate consciousnesses. You tell me that you exist, and I exist, so now there're two of us...

Well, what's YOUR experience? What do YOU know for sure?

-I'm here. I exist.

Do you know anything about me, in terms of my existence? Where does my existence happen as far as you know?

-In the consciousness that I am.

In YOUR experience. In YOUR consciousness. The only thing you can know is your consciousness, your experience. Everything "else" is a guess, a hypothesis. Right?

-So outside of my consciousness, I don't know that you exist. Nothing is happening outside of my consciousness.

Of course! How could it be? Look for yourself. How could you possibly know anything outside of your consciousness?

-So my thinking other people exist is just a pattern in my consciousness...

Of course. When you go to sleep and you dream, you may think you're seeing all kinds of people running around doing all kinds of things. When you wake up in the morning, in that context it's obvious that there was no one there in the dream but you. Right?

-I get the dream analogy, but where it doesn't work for me is I've never dreamed the same thing twice...

If you notice carefully, you've never had the same experience twice when you're awake either, have you?

-But, I recognize you when I see you...

You think you do. You recognize people in your dreams, too. Are they there? The recognition is something that happens subjectively in your consciousness. It's energy appearing in your consciousness. Have you EVER had an experience that wasn't energy appearing in your consciousness?

-...No.

So what reality can be said to consist of as far as you know, is energy appearing in your consciousness. Right?

-Right. And that's it?

Stay there. Where else is there to go? And you ARE that consciousness. Because anything "else" that appears in that consciousness, is dependent on that consciousness for its appearance to appear. Like your body is in your consciousness, this ipod is in your consciousness, or this room is in your consciousness; but the constant in the equation is always "your" consciousness. You go to sleep and your body disappears, but the consciousness that it was appearing in is still there. So what you are is the consciousness, not any partial experience that is appearing in it. It's obvious. This is the result of asking "What can we know for SURE", as opposed to what is speculation. We can speculate all we want. I can suppose that you all exist as somehow more than energies in my experience, but the fact is, based on the evidence, I can't possibly know that. What I can know is "you" AS ENERGY appearing in "my" consciousness. That's where I start and that's where I end. Any other supposition is fine, but it's just supposition. It's just a hypotheses. I can suppose, "Maybe you DO exist in the same way that I exist and are having your own experience"; and having the nature I do I may be motivated to talk with you about all this stuff to try to be of benefit, or because it amuses me to do so. But it's all a mystery ultimately.

All I'm recommending is not to leap to conclusions. To stay with what is the CERTAINTY, what is the bedrock of truth that we can rest on. What is that fact? There IS a fact. There's definitely a fact. And that fact is the being of the present moment. The "isness" of the present moment, which I subsequently analyze as consisting of energy in consciousness. But even that's speculation right there; because what do those words mean? What is consciousness actually? What is energy? I do that as a device to try to indicate what's going on, but it's fundamentally not accurate; you have to look and see for yourself what actually IS going on right here right now, to try to see what those words are actually referring to.

What then IS the truth? It can't be said. The truth is "IS", "SAT" in Sanskrit, which means being, truth, isness; what actually is.

-Our ego isn't just our identity, it's the whole construct that we think the world is?

ANY construct is ego. What's actually existing is pure beingness; that's the reality. Anything whatsoever that is abstracted from that primal fact as an idea, belief, or supposition, is ego. Any models. And we use those models to create a story, the story of what we are and what our life is. The elements that make up the story are the supposed "things" that we think exist; our bodies, other people, objects, cities, society, the solar system, every "thing". The story of all this presupposes that these "things", the elements that make up the story, actually exist; whereas in reality they are just imaginary concepts that we've abstracted out of this infinite, indefinable Being.

All those supposed elements we use to build a story, and the very act of building that story, is egoism. And that's all that traps us, when we get trapped. We build these elaborate stories in imagination and then we identify with them, we think we're IN these stories, and then we think we're STUCK in those stories. Once you see that all the elements that your story is made of don't actually exist as objective realities in the way you think they do, then your whole story collapses; and where does that leave you? You don't know where you are, you don't know what you are; but then there's nothing to trap you, and no you to be trapped. THIS is liberation. THIS is enlightenment; simply seeing that there is in actuality nothing that can possibly trap you, and no separable you that could be trapped.

And all that is the sense in which it's said in many spiritual traditions that ego is the enemy of realization.

-So those are the invisible bars you talk about, that once you see what they're made of, they can't trap you...

Yes. Because the bars are made out of consciousness itself, they're made out of ideas. The things that we think trap us, they aren't THINGS. Once we see they're not things, we see we can't be trapped by them. They're made of nothing but consciousness. We're nothing but consciousness; how can consciousness be trapped by consciousness?

They're just hypotheses. They're just "what if's". "Well, WHAT IF I was something called a human being and I was breathing stuff called air and I was living on something called a planet, with all sorts of complex situations involving supposed other "things" and "people" going on on it, that somehow might involve me..." It's a perfectly plausible story, and it's one possible interpretation of events; but it's PURELY hypothetical.

The fact is since we CAN'T know anything for certain about the actual reality that we're deriving those abstractions from, pure being, then the abstractions collapse as certainties, as reliable realities. They're only guesswork; and CERTAIN to be inaccurate since they're all FINITE ideas, but derived from an INFINITE source that they can't possibly capture.

Simply, you can't start from something that you don't know what it is, and meaningfully derive from that something that you DO know what it is. And we CAN'T know what reality is. We KNOW nothing BUT IT, but we can't say what that IS. So all our ideas about it, from which we fashion these elaborate, heroic, and tragic stories, are pure guesswork.

-I seem to be getting more forgetful; is there anything about this that would make me forgetful?

Well, everything you can remember is fundamentally a lie anyways. So if you're in a state of forgetfulness, you're actually experiencing the reality of your being. Every instant is new and it hasn't happened before. Anything you want to remember isn't really a "thing".

The bottom line is we don't have any control. If you remember something you remember it, if you don't you don't. You didn't remember it on purpose, and you didn't forget it on purpose. If you lose your keys you lose your keys; and if you find them again, then that's what happens. It's just the flow of being.

There's only one thing that's important to remember; and that's the ongoing flow of being. IT'S really impossible to forget, since there's nothing else; but we can forget that we're seeing it if we get caught up in all sorts of stories and ideas that we think are actual. We haven't really forgotten it, we're just misinterpreting it as being all this stuff.

-I've heard that we are exposed to billions of bits of information every second, but our brains only have the power to process thousands or millions...

Yes, that filtering is very easy to see in realtime, and that's a very valuable thing to do. If you look at the experience that you're having right now, there are certain things you're thinking, certain things you're feeling, certain things you're aware of as your senses. But if you notice carefully, at the same time there's a whole vast sea of weird background "noise"; and we're in the habit of discarding this noise because we think it's not important, that it has no meaningful content. We may think it's extraneous nerve firings in our retinas, white noise behind our thoughts, etc..

It's like looking at a bad print of a video where you can piece out the action, but there's all this other static and snow, and we're in the habit of just focusing on the action and ignoring the noise. BUT that noise is actual realtime experience, spontaneously emerging from Universal Intelligence. It inherently has content, it has meaning, it has value as much as any real experience.

-So how do you know what to pick?

DON'T! Stop picking. Become aware of all your real experience as it is. Experience the full field of your experience, and you're experiencing your full reality.

-So how do you remove the filters, to experience all our actual experience?

Just notice it. Meditate, contemplate, investigate your experiencing. Meditation is a classic example. When people sit to meditate, not any elaborate meditation but just to sit and watch your thoughts, you start to notice all of a sudden that there's all this crap there. Notice the crap! Don't think of the crap as being a problem or something you're supposed to stop, notice it! Let it grow. Notice the full field of what you're ACTUALLY experiencing in realtime. It's really not hard to do, but we're habituated to NOT noticing. We're habituated to thinking that only a narrow range of people and objects in our experience matter, and that all this other information is noise and DOESN'T matter. The fact that this particular thread in this rug here, for example, is sort of an off brown, and the one next to it appears to be an extremely similar but different shade doesn't seem important, so I ignore it. But then I might think you guys matter, because you might think certain things about me and I might want to impress you and be socially acceptable to gain fulfillment for myself.

That's the sort of utilitarian mental programming that we usually operate under. It's goal oriented. We select the aspects of our experience that we think are going to get us points: get us money, get us attention, get us love, get us whatever our story implies we need to feel happy, to feel whole.

-In short, we're always living in the future, anticipating future rewards for our actions...

Right. But the present also contains all that OTHER information which is being ignored, studiously ignored. And it's not that it's not there clearly perceivable, we're just looking away from it. It's like being in a dark room where there's a flashlight shining on one spot, leaving the rest of the room in indistinct, but not total, darkness. There are all sorts of relatively indistinct things to see in the room, noise, but that one spot is what's being illuminated, so that's what we look at. And we ignore the fact that there's all this other "less distinct" stuff around.

But it's not that we can't SEE it, we're just ignoring it. And it's just about noticing that we're ignoring it; and that very noticing will open our awareness to be able to experience it, and we'll open to the fullness of our experience in realtime, to WHAT we truly are.

-You mean, we should FOCUS on the things we've been ignoring?

Well you can explore and play with focussing, but generally speaking focus is our enemy, because what you're calling focus is mostly actually filtering, blocking the entirety of our reality.

-The goal oriented thing again.

Yeah, we ALREADY know how to do that, this is an experiment to look and see if we can discover other approaches than that to our reality. To see the aspects of our experience that we're used to throwing out with the garbage. And the point is, if we open COMPLETELY to the fullness of our experience in realtime as it is, we are seeing reality. Period. There IS nothing more beyond this, this is the absolute. This is God. This is Tao/Teh. This is the Trikaya.

-Then there's no choosing what's going to happen next...

Right, there's no choosing, of course there's no choosing. What does choosing consist of? When you start to open to the full field of your experience, you start to be able to look at what is REALLY happening as "things" are happening, rather than just defining them, like "I'm making a choice." What is actually happening when I think I'm making a choice? Urges spontaneously arise in consciousness, thoughts arise, interpretations arise... Where do they arise from? Before they've arisen, do you decide that they're GOING to arise? Do you MAKE them arise? THAT would really be the exercise of choice. But if you look carefully at any process of choice, what we call an act of choice is the after-the-fact labeling of a situation where urges and thoughts have actually spontaneously appeared from nowhere.

Thoughts come from, and disappear to, nowhere. We think that WE'RE thinking thoughts, but in actuality we DON'T think about thinking the particular thoughts before we think them, or decide before we think them that we're GOING to think them; in actuality the thoughts just pop up, and THEN we identify that we're thinking them.

-They just show up.

Well yeah, look and see for yourself. For example, I'm thinking of a tree right now. And I can say I'm thinking of a tree because I AM thinking of a tree. But did I think I was going to think about a tree before the thought of the tree appeared in my awareness? Did I decide I was going to have the thought of the tree before I had the thought of the tree? If you look carefully, it's all just the spontaneous eruption of energy in consciousness, and then we spin doctor it, saying "Oh, I'M thinking about this, I'M thinking about that, I'M deciding this; but the deciding actually happens spontaneously before the fact of our claiming it, in the miraculous, unstoppable bubbling forth of all this energy in consciousness.

And it's the same with perception. I don't decide to see what I'm seeing in the moment, it just shows up. There it is! You know? Right now here you all are, here is this room, here is this rug. I'm calling it you all and the room and the rug, but that naming is of course completely arbitrary, in actuality it's just this field of undefinable, constantly changing varieties of energy spontaneously appearing and simultaneously disappearing in consciousness. It's entirely AMAZING.

But the point is to open to experiencing it AS IT IS, rather than just settling for our accustomed models and labels of what we're used to thinking it is, because that's just dumbing ourselves down. You know, I might think "I'm a guy and I'm doing this and that, and my goals are such and such, and I'm sitting here in this place and I'm getting kind of bored, maybe I'll take off and go have a beer." All that may be TRUE, on ONE level, but there's so, so, so much more that's also in the reality of my experience that I'm ignoring by that storyline. So if I settle for that storyline I'm lying to myself. I'm oversimplifying. I'm taking an infinitely complex situation manifested by absolute universal intelligence and turning it into a simple cartoon.

And maybe, if I open to that infinite complexity, there's something enormously valuable there that I'm missing. THAT'S the point. When we open to what our consciousness actually IS, by looking at its full expression, we might find out that, "Oh my God! This consciousness is actually everything; and I AM that consciousness. I don't exist in the WORLD, the world exists IN THIS CONSCIOUSNESS and I am that consciousness."

It's an obvious fact, but to see it we have to SEE it. We have to look around the tree trunks of our usual obsessions to see the forest that it actually is.

Desire is the upwelling of the divine force. Literally. Like everything is. Like all sensation is. When you see something, it's the upwelling of the divine force. When you think something, when you feel something, when you feel a desire. All sensory experience, all mental experience, is pure Shakti, pure divine energy. It's the spotlight of God shining out of itself. God is radiant by nature. Radiant as well as perceptive. Everything IS this radiance, and this radiance is pure ecstasy, pure energy. It's like fireworks, you know? It's the big bang. And it's always happening, there's nothing but. It's pure ecstasy.

-So the radiance is the light on the screen of perception.

Well, yeah, there's nothing BUT radiance, there's nothing BUT perception. We can use these two words, but they are one. The actuality of reality is indescribable; the perception IS radiant in itself, the radiance IS perceptive; and they both are the entirety of God. The texture of experience is itself the radiance. It is presence. It is the divine force. Every experience we have, every sound we hear, every sight we see, every thought we think, is a bursting forth of mysterious energy into present consciousness. And WHAT is bursting forth is of course consciousness itself. And what's PERCEIVING it is also consciousness itself. And what it's MADE of is consciousness itself.

And seeing that fact is getting a true perspective on what all this is, on what's happening right here, right now. And then from that perspective we can play with different models or play with desires or do whatever the hell we want, because they aren't entrapping anymore; because we see what they really are. They're ALL just divine energy; and there's no individual person to be entrapped anyway. You can't entrap God; it ain't gonna happen. Only God can do that. (Laughter)

And we are ourselves in the final analysis nothing but God; so how can we be entrapped?

-Then when I'm scared or something, it's just a reflex...

It's karma, the patterning of the flow of things, the ongoing expression of the energies that you are. The play goes on; Alex will continue to be Alex. But the WAY Alex is is the result of all the chaotic programming that makes him what he is. The genetic heritage and all the environmental accidents that have shaped him into what he is, functionally. So he's basically a reactor; he reacts to the situations that he perceives going on around him, in accordance with the way his temperament, his personality, his karma, dictates. Right?

But what does that have to do with YOU? And what relationship to all that does the fact that you are the disembodied consciousness that's EXPERIENCING it have? Look and see, look at that. What's experiencing you, WHAT'S looking through your eyes RIGHT NOW? It's what you ARE, isn't it?

-Yeah, and it's aware of everything (laughs)

Yes, it's aware of it all. Look and see what your relationship to "things" is. If you are the consciousness that experiences your experience, everything you experience must be in you, or how could you experience it? In other words, what you're experiencing has to be IN your consciousness for you to experience it. Right? And if you ARE that consciousness, then everything is IN YOU. The universe is IN YOU. So, you are everything. Just exactly like in a dream. In a dream, everything that happens, including the environments, the characters, your embodiment in the dream, everything, is appearing WITHIN the dreaming consciousness that you actually are; the dreamer. Right? And the dreamer itself is not affected by what appears to happen in the dream. But what happens in the dream is CLEARLY the dreamer and nothing but. You know?

But exactly the same relationship exists, I suggest, between you and your experience now in the "waking" state, and actually in ALL states, as in a dream. It's easy to see it in the dream from the waking state since you're looking at it from outside the dream now, and you can see it from an outside perspective and notice "Oh! It was a dream!" But it's harder to see from outside of THIS dream, because we don't have an immediate and obvious experience from outside of it.

But you CAN see from outside; you ARE now and always do. You just have to come to KNOW that you can, and not be hypnotized into thinking that you CAN'T by your belief that you're IN it.

-But there is no outside...

Right. Outside is just a turn of phrase. Outside as opposed to not trapped within it. Experience happens WITHIN consciousness. Consciousness is not stuck within the experience. The details of experience depend on consciousness, consciousness does not depend on the details of experience. When the experience changes, the consciousness doesn't change.

If you got really sick now and had a 105 degree fever, you would get delirious and groggy; but you would KNOW that with absolute clarity, because the consciousness would not have a fever. Consciousness ITSELF would not be sick; even as it experiences a sick body in the field of its experience. And clearly that's what you ACTUALLY are, even though you as that consciousness are experiencing being a sick person. Do you see the relationship? Look at it. Look at what's looking out of your eyes right now. It's in real time, it's NOT a concept; you can actually look and see what it is. And WHAT sees what it is, IS what's looking out of your eyes; that's what sees everything.

This is all so obvious once you see it. It's a miracle that most people seem to be unable to see it. It's so obvious.

What's experiencing your experience right now? We're so used to thinking, "Oh, my body is". But the body is clearly an object IN our experience. What's experiencing the experience? It's totally close and obvious in realtime.

-So what about when an event happens, and it shifts my state, like from being very happy to being unhappy...

Of course. It happens all the time, nonstop. But that's just ONE possible description of experience, right? We're constantly being moved through various mental states and emotional states as a reaction to our interpretation of experiences as they arise. The experiences arise mysteriously; we can't determine what they're made of or where they come from, or even where they ARE. Our ideas about it all arise mysteriously as well. We tend to own our thoughts, and think "I'M thinking this" or "I'M thinking that". But if you look very closely, I think you'll find that thoughts just sort of pop out of nowhere, unbidden. And emotions likewise, they just sort of come and go; so both the events, and our reactions to them, are all just this spontaneous cascading of the unknown through consciousness. So what do you do with that? What do you do with that... Anything you want! (laughter) Because whatever you DO do, will just be more of THAT. It's nonstop.

-Sounds like a lot of movement.

Well maybe yes, maybe no. Maybe it's not movement at all, maybe it's like a dream where there's actually no movement whatsoever. It's energy in consciousness. One way to understand experience is that it's countless discrete flashes of energy that flash instantaneously in consciousness, then to be replaced by other flashes, and so on. Like if you watch TV and watch someone apparently walk across a room, there's no movement happening at all; there are just different stationary flashes of light, that imply an interpretation of motion where there isn't any.

And it may be that the world is like that. It may be that there is no motion whatsoever, just non-spatial flashes of quantum energy; and through our free association of interpretation we interpret it as movement, or stability, or chaos, or order; whatever. But it may all be just the same thing. Who can say?

But all of this is just models of something that is fundamentally unmodelable. As near as I can tell, the fact is we can't know WHAT'S going on, with any certainty, in terms of modeling it. On the other hand, we can know NOTHING OTHER than what it IS, in terms of experiencing it. Because our experience IS it. It's in our face, 24/7.

-So we know it, but it's still so subject to interpretation.

Exactly. We can know it, but we can't know WHAT it is. And when we start interpreting it, we're sunk. We have free rein in interpreting, and most of us exercise that with wild abandon. But the problem is if we aren't aware that we're doing it, if we aren't aware of the arbitrary nature of our interpreting, we're liable to find ourselves creating fantastic worlds that don't correlate to reality. We're liable to create some big soap opera that we think is our life and then we start thinking we're failures, or start punishing ourselves for not achieving something, or we think we're successful and we start to get greedy and try to hang on to it in the face of the fact that everything is constantly changing.

And then we're basically screwed, thinking we live in a world with no escape.

-It's incredible that there's experience at all...

It's incredible, amazing. The whole thing is completely miraculous. That's why it's called God; it's beyond explanation, it's totally beyond any human modeling. It's infinite, indescribable. BUT it's what we actually are. We have massive conceptual inferiority complexes. We think we're these little primates running around in this maze-like world, but that's an absurdity. We're God. We're outside the whole system. WE'RE what the whole system is made of.

I think culturally it has been made into a taboo to think that; you're not supposed to think you're god. God is supposed to be "out there", so inconceivably great, and we tiny creatures are supposed to grovel before it. And it IS amazing, unfathomable; but it's what we ARE in actuality. It's what everything is. Calling it "we" is arbitrary; it's what this rug is, it's what this body is, it's what this personality is, it's what the air is, it's what the light is... It's what EVERYTHING is.

But there's no ME other than it; so it's what I am. I AM THAT.

- So, there's consciousness that's not dependent on phenomena, but you're saying that the energy that is the phenomena is also that consciousness? So the observer IS the observed?

Yeah. Look at a dream. What are the "things" in a dream made of? You can have really elaborate dreams that seem totally real. I don't know if you've had lucid dreams to verify this clearly, but you can have dreams that are exactly as real-seeming and detailed as this experience we're having right here. Then what's it all made of? When you wake up, it's gone, and turns out never to have existed in actuality. Where did it go? Where did it come from when it appeared? What was it made of while it was there? Clearly it was made of the consciousness, projected by consciousness, made of the dreaming itself.

What experience is made of as far as we can know is consciousness, because our experience is of consciousness and in consciousness. Even if there WAS some kind of objectivity outside of consciousness we couldn't KNOW it, because we can only experience what's in our consciousness.

-I'm not sure I followed that...

Suppose there was something outside of consciousness that's causing our experience, some objective world, say matter; and it interacts with consciousness and causes this experience to occur. Since we CAN'T know whether or not that's the case, it becomes a moot point. We can't know that there's matter; all we CAN know is that there's experience. So it becomes a closed system, which is in actuality what we are.

We can't know anything outside of our consciousness, so it's idle speculation whether or not there IS anything "out there", like wondering how many angels can dance on the head of a pin.

-So to call it "energy in consciousness" is speculation?

No, "energy in consciousness" is a close description of the actual fact; that there's anything ELSE is speculation. So everything whatsoever boils down to just being energy in consciousness as far as we're concerned.

-But then those two things are one, right?

Of course! They are approximate descriptions of the one inscrutable fact that constitutes reality. Although calling it "one" or "many" is meaningless.

-We only know the energy WITH consciousness?

Of course, they coexist; where there's what we're calling consciousness there's always what we're calling energy, and where there's energy there's always consciousness.

-How would you know that you were there if there wasn't energy?

Yes, that's right on the money. And EVERYTHING collapses down to THAT, the truth we're trying to indicate by calling it "consciousness in energy". Period. It's just our Being as it is. Calling it consciousness and energy, or calling it ANYTHING, is arbitrary.

-So if you were to summarize in one statement what is true...

SAT, period. IS.

-But "you" is, or just "is" is?

IS is. The idea that "I am" is an assumption derived after the fact, which is the naked and primal fact that BEING IS. This is an important point. But I AM that "isness" in actuality. I AM THAT. What else could I be? What else is there? ANYTHING that "is", is that. Because any "thing" is BEING, so consists of THAT itself in terms of what it actually is.

It's difficult to talk about, but the point is NOT to talk about it, but to look and see for yourself. SEE what it is. How many things are happening here that you know for sure?

-The only thing I know for sure is that I'm experiencing.

Yeah. Exactly. And even saying that it's "you" experiencing is a construct of language. What you really know is that EXPERIENCE IS. And because experience is, we can abstract out or derive the idea that, "Well, there's a me that's experiencing it"; but that "me" is just a mental idea. Because the primary fact is that experience is happening; and it's from THAT fact that we derive the idea that there's a "me" experiencing it. And then if there's a "me" that's experiencing, there might be a "something" that I'm experiencing, and the idea of "the world" is born.

But both "me" and "the world" have been abstracted in the imagination by consciousness out of the fundamental naked fact of ISNESS, which alone is NOT imaginary.

-Which goes back to the idea that reality is really one system, which the appearance of all "things" and "actions" are produced by, and can't be separated out from...

Yes. And of course even calling it a "system" is an abstraction. That's just a way of indication that its functioning is producing the appearance of all this as experience. Being appears to be all this, while not actually being anything other than the pure being that it is. HOW does it do that? It's a miracle. It's the fundamental mystery. God is a mystery, and that is God, this being of the present moment. This experience that's happening now, is the absolute. And it's concrete and obvious, even as all our ideas and suppositions about it are subtle and devious, abstract and all highly suspect.

But we have it all backwards, usually! We think the shaky devious suppositions in our imaginations are what's solid, and that this solid reality of experiencing as it is is abstract, because it seems so infinite and we can't pin it down. But hey, that's just what it is! Maybe it's just infinite and you can't pin it down! What do you do with that?

-I seem to feel a strong urge to serve others...

If the urge to serve arises in you, then that's part of what you ARE. And it's the universal expression manifesting as you, as that in those circumstances. The urge for it actually comes from the mystery. What's the source of it? Where does it come from? You can't trace it back to a fixed location. So, again, it's an expression of the universe. It's an expression of what you ACTUALLY are. Different people have different urges that show up in different ways at different points in their lives, and on and on. But NONE of it is ours. There's NO entity that's us that's separable from the stream of our manifestation, which DOESN'T come FROM us. WE aren't making our manifestation. Manifestation is upwelling and we are that upwelling! And the whole universe is that upwelling. It's all an absolutely direct expression of God, the Divine Being. Everything. Even what we are owning and identifying with and struggling with and working on and effecting and resisting and all that. All that machination simply IS, WE didn't decide to do that. It's a natural upwelling of, a natural expression of the universe as us.

There's no US, there's just the system of what reality is; there's the basis, the ground which upwells as all expressions of that ground, that we call experience. And then all subsequent definitions and entities that we define into existence conceptually, they aren't actually there. There's no basis for their separate existence in reality. There's just the upwelling of consciousness in consciousness. Our bodies functioning is part of the upwelling. It all simply IS. But it's all ultimately absolutely impersonal (or ultimately absolutely personal, to look at it from another point of view).

All maps are false, because Reality is unmappable. Reality is infinite, even as it is immediate, obvious and closer than the closest thing there is to you. It's what you ARE. It's your very nature. So there's actually no distance whatever between it and you.

Examine the present moment. How long does it last? There's no answer that you're going to get that's formulatable, because Reality isn't an answer. It's a bottomless infinity. But looking at it most directly, most closely, most intently is how you see it. As the present vanishes into the past and the future moves into the present, what's going on in that mechanism? It's always happening. It's completely obvious, but it's only not obvious because we don't look at it because we're used to looking at our models. We're looking at our models instead of looking at the thing ITSELF.

When you are thinking of the past, WHEN are you thinking of it? In THIS moment, so the past doesn't exist except in the present moment. When are you thinking about the future, what does that thinking of it actually consist?

What are thoughts? Look at them. WHAT are they? Thoughts have no duration. Thoughts are a part of the flow of time. They appear and simultaneously they seem to vanish and a new thought comes in. What's up with that? Look at it. It's readily apparent. It's right in our face constantly. Look at it intimately. What is it?

It's a matter of being a scientist, saying "Okay, I don't know what's going on. Let me try and figure it out. What's the raw data?" Well, the raw data is that experience seems to be happening. I don't have a CLUE what that ACTUALLY means, but we'll call it experience and that it seems to be happening, whatever THOSE two words mean. Examine that closely, experientially, not conceptually. Look at what it really is.

Go into your experience; you ARE your experience. Embrace it, texturally. Hug it. Feel it. Your experience is like a tub of warm jello. Feel it, go into it. Don't model it or pick it apart or analyze it. Just BE it. Feel what it feels like. What does time feel like? The passage of time has a texture. It's amazing! FEEL it. We usually don't notice what it actually is because we're thinking of our models. Space has a texture, being itself has a texture.

We were talking earlier about the bardos; and we were discussing how the whole bardo teachings actually apply to our current situation, not just to some supposed afterlife. I don't know if you're familiar with the bardo teachings?

-No, what are they?

Simplistically put, the bardo teachings (of Tibetan Buddhism) state that once you die, first of all a state of darkness is experienced, of nescience. Then a state of "clear light" is experienced, pure unqualified awareness itself; then you will progressively experience states where various visions are experienced. And the bardo teachings state that if you get sucked in to believing in the independent reality of the visions you're experiencing, having emotional reactions of hope and fear with regard to them, you're screwed. The antidote to this entrapment is to either stay with the clear light, or to see that the visions are themselves the clear light. Which is exactly what you hear me recommending here; to see what our experience is made of. What is it? Where is it happening? We get hypnotized into thinking that there's a material world that's objective, and we're in some relationship to it, and we're some tiny primate creature running around at the mercy of circumstances.

But is that true? Our first-person evidence is that in actual fact, all of experience happens in ME. All of experience happens in my consciousness. And it's all made of unfathomable energy. This is exactly akin to what the bardo teachings indicate.

If you see the truth of that, then what can trap you? You'd be being trapped by what is essentially light. If some circumstance seems to trap you, you're being trapped by pure energy in divine consciousness. So how trapped can you be?

The full bardo teachings are that EVERY state of experience is a bardo state, so ultimately the same recommendations as to how to deal with them apply across the board. So the teaching is not just applying to what happens after you die, it's about what's happening RIGHT NOW.

THIS is pure consciousness; and if we see that, we get to celebrate it! If we don't see that, then we may think we're stuck in whatever erroneous interpretation our demented imaginations and programming have come up with.

-How can we know what happens after death?

How can we know what's happening right now? I say work with what you can, and what you can is what's right here, right now. What is THIS? If you want to find God, if you want to understand reality, the best place to look is RIGHT HERE. Start HERE, and see what THIS is.

-And this actually is that clear light?

Well, look and see. Is it? If you can see for yourself that it is, then that's it; game over. What are we made of? What ARE we?

-Then where is there to go? There isn't, there's just this...

It's THIS, this here and now. And what IS this? What is it, what is it...

-Sometimes people talk to me about what it will be like when we die...

We have such a fertile field for investigation right here right now, so, frittering our efforts away trying to investigate speculative hypothetical possibilities; what's the point? If you KNOW what's going on right here right now, THEN you can afford to take the time to speculate.

But any state of experience has to boil down to being the same thing that's happening right now; infinite energy in consciousness. This is EVERYTHING. But what actually is "energy"? What is "consciousness"? But even if we let those questions go, life is energy in consciousness, so death has to be energy in consciousness.

But that's all irrelevant, because it's just conceptualizations. What is conceptualization? Energy in consciousness. And when does conceptualization always happen?

-Now...

It's just you interacting with your karma, the play of the energies that you ARE. Everything and everyone that you experience is a convenient enactment of your karma, like in a dream. Everyone shows up in your life as a convenient extra on the set of the "You Show", and they are all fulfilling exactly the role you need them to, for the "You Show" to be what it is. As the plot of the "You Show" develops, the characters in the show develop or drop out and new ones will come in. It's all subjective. You're not "moving through" because there's nothing there to move through. It moves through YOU if anything. It's you moving through you. It's your pattern of yourself, your karma moving through your consciousness. And everything that you see is just a depiction of that, exactly like a dream. When you go to sleep and dream, there are all these various forms, and very elaborate involvements, all of which are just a depiction of meanings that are important to you on an intimate level. So it's not like there's anything there that you're moving through. It's more like, you're there, and your "youness" is showing up as all of this display.

All we experience is our own karma, the energies of our own nature. So you're just experiencing yourself. And it looks like this cast of thousands and this elaborate play. All of that, if you look at it very closely, is all you. It's just energy in your consciousness. I can assume that you all exist, but I can't POSSIBLY verify it. It will always remain an assumption. What I CAN know is that you ARE. I can know that you are in my life because it's a depiction of my life at this moment. And likewise, I'm in your life, because it's a depiction of your life at this moment. What I am to you is different than what you are to me, because my life is different than your life.

In other words, I'm dreaming. I'm dreaming you all. You ALSO may be dreaming and dreaming us all, but they're two different dreams. We're each experiencing our karma unfolding.

We're habituated into inhabiting specialized areas of our experience that we call home, where we feel comfortable. "My home is my thoughts, and I know that room really well and I go there and I hang out... there IS this whole city which is the fullness of my experience, but I like to hang out in this room because this is my room and I'm safe here". That's ego. The more we break that habit, the more we inhabit the actual fullness of our experience, the more we're opening to what we REALLY are, as opposed to some specialized part of what we are that we're comfortable with, or that we're at home with.

Children know it all. THEN they get inculturated with all this bullshit and unnecessarily complicated conceptualizations, which are absolutely not true. But they get seduced into believing that they ARE true, then they're in conflict and denying their own intuition, which is hopelessly confusing. They KNOW intuitively that they know the truth, but they've been taught that THAT truth isn't the truth and THIS truth is; and none of it makes any sense and they know intuitively it isn't true, but they have to somehow MAKE it true and it's just a hopeless struggle. And it ends up with all the psychotic and neurotic humans that are running around on the earth believing all these crazy ideas... but it's all part of the process. It seems to be part of the process of individual human evolution for consciousness to forget itself and then remember itself.

Thinking is just one small layer of our experience. It's as important as it is big, and it's NOT very big. Our experience is this vast sea of energy. We break it up into sight, sound, touch, smell, thinking, feeling, other sorts of more amorphous mental experiences, and perhaps even MORE amorphous subtle deep experiences. It's arbitrary how many layers you want to conceptually slice it up into. But its totality is this vast sea of energy, constantly metamorphosing, made up of patterns of light and energies of experience.

As a whole, IT is what is important. All importance is embodied in it, but if you're focusing on one tiny little piece of it, you're missing the whole picture. You're getting a partial view of things. And it's in COMPLETENESS that you feel the fullness, the wholeness of your true being. So try not to let yourself get tunnel vision and be pulled into one tiny piece of your experience... your thoughts, your feelings, or anything. Notice the whole of it. Even as you're thinking, you're also seeing... feel that. You're also smelling. You're also having emotions, you're having all sorts of mental experiences of sparkles and whirls and things going on in the background that we don't even acknowledge they're there, because we get fixated on the thoughts, or whatever we're obsessed with. It's like overspecialization.

THIS is a miracle! What is it? Where is it? It's consciousness that seems to be appearing from where? From nowhere, from itself. Look and see for yourself right now. What is it in? What sort of space is it in? We can't say, how can we say? But if we can look and try to see directly what kind of space it is in, then we can SEE the miracle, see the fact that this being is actually based ONLY IN ITSELF. The whole universe appears only in itself ; but if you really look at what that implies, what it means, it is ungraspable conceptually. But, it's totally obvious and totally immediate when you open yourself to experiencing it non conceptually.

EMBODIMENT

We are not in our bodies, our bodies are in us.

-Our bodies are in us?

Yeah. I'll give you an example. I'll explain the perspective. Suppose you're dreaming at night, and you're dreaming that you're walking down the street. Now you aren't actually IN the body that's walking down the street, are you? The body that's walking down the street is in you, which is the you that actually exists as the dreaming consciousness.

And exactly the same relationship exists between our bodies NOW and consciousness. Our consciousness is the field of our experience in which our bodies, and everything, appears. For example if you cut off you hand, you haven't lost a piece of your consciousness. It may be more subtle to see, but even if you're anesthetized you don't lose a piece of your consciousness. Your experience changes drastically, but it's not like your consciousness stops existing. Or the same in deep sleep; again, that's a subtle thing to observe because we're not being generally very aware of that, but in deep sleep our consciousness is there. The consciousness is the being. Consciousness is identical with being and being persists in deep sleep. We wake up in the morning, we don't feel like "Oh I've just been created." There's still a sense of continuity that we have preexisted.

When does ANY experience always happen? Now. It's already a done deal. Just look and see what it IS. What it is, where it is... And it turns out to be what WE are, because all our ideas of ourselves are derived from IT. Our ideas of ourselves are abstract concepts and imaginary modelings which are derived from this completely mysterious being that is happening right here right now.

That's always the way we are; we aren't IN our bodies, our bodies are in us, in our consciousness. My hand is in my consciousness. WHERE is it? It's out here in consciousness, or in here in consciousness. Where's my body? In here in consciousness. Take a minute and feel the entire feeling of your body from top to bottom, just the full field of your sense of touch, right now.

Where is that experience happening? It's happening IN the field of consciousness. Isn't it? So our bodies exist IN our consciousness, our consciousness doesn't exist in our body.

And we ARE that consciousness. There's no reason to expect that it's going to be any different whether our body is around or not. I mean, we go to sleep at night and our body vanishes. We dream and we have a whole new body in our consciousness. Which is the real body, if any?

- Even sitting, sometimes there's no body...

Sure. There never IS any body, there's just energy in consciousness. We may interpret the energy appearing to be "there's my hand, there's my body, there's your body, there's this room" (points), but those differentiations are largely arbitrary. Because you can't pin down what any of it is definitively. So I can say "that's the room" (points), but what exactly is the room? Can I draw a circle around it?

Can I say "This exactly is the room" and nothing else? I can't, because it's infinite and open-ended, and exists only in my experience. So there is no one simple thing that I can point to and say it is the room. There's no one simple thing I can point to and say "There's my body", there's no one simple thing I can point to and say there's ANYTHING.

So all this differentiating is all a cloud of speculation, essentially. But at the same time, it's IMMEDIATELY PRESENT IN CONSCIOUSNESS as consciousness. There's nothing but, that we can find. Consciousness keeps washing through itself; and we may play at all this differentiating, in consciousness, but it's all hypothetical.

You know, it's like watching a TV, and thinking you're seeing people walking around in the world that seems to be in the TV - but in actuality you're just seeing dots of light. There're no people, there's no room, there's no situation; there're just little instantaneous flashes of light. And that's exactly the same thing that's happening right now; I'm seeing little flashes of light.

Space has a texture, Being itself has a texture. When you're feeling that, you're feeling your own embodiment. Your embodiment is time. Your embodiment is space. I mean your body as Consciousness in Form. It has all of these very intimate, very obvious sensory qualities that we can perceive very directly if we open to them intimately. They're texture.

Being is a sensual experience above all else. OPEN to that sensuality. OPEN to the texture of it. The lusciousness of it. And that in itself will teach us a lot about what it is. It might not be a rational or a linear kind of logic that it's teaching us... but it's pregnant with intelligence. It's pregnant with pure infinite intelligence, so as such, it is teaching us, showing us what IT is.

-But we tend to CARE what happens to us, and want things to go a certain way...

That's due to an investment in an imaginary incomplete self-image. We have a deep, maybe unconscious belief that we are a certain way, that we live in a world that is a certain way, a sort of cartoon we carry around in our mind, imaging that we're incomplete. We may think we're a little monkey-person and there're other monkey-people "out there" that are better than us; and we think, "Wouldn't it be nice if we were like them; and gosh, if we could just figure out the right way to do it we could be one of them, and THEN we would be fulfilled".

It's a whole cartoon that plays itself out in our imaginations, but it's based on false assumptions. Because we AREN'T little monkey-people. We SEE little monkey-people in our experience; I look in the mirror and I see a monkey, but WHAT is seeing that is this consciousness that miraculously appears from nowhere, and THAT'S what we really are. When I go to sleep at night the monkey disappears, but that miraculous consciousness is still there. THAT'S what we are; that's our true self, that's our true self image. That's "your face before you were born". And if we had THAT as our self image, where would our problem be? The fact that these little monkey-people are running around in the perceptions of our consciousness is just a phenomena like the weather, who cares? But when we think WE'RE one of the monkeys, all of a sudden it's "Oh my god, I'm just a little monkey in a big scary world... what am I going to do?".

-So the problem is holding an untrue self image?

Yes. Pure and simple. If we have a self image which accurately reflects what our ACTUAL self is, we would see that we are complete, we are inviolable, we lack nothing, we are eternal, we can't die, we can't be born; so in that context, the concept of "a problem" can't exist meaningfully. But that's a framework that we generally don't have, ONLY because we are invested in other imaginary frameworks. But the point is to examine those other conceptual frameworks, and SEE if they're true, SEE if the evidence supports them, or if they're based on assumptions that aren't verifiable in the reality of our experience.

It's manifestly obvious that consciousness appears from nowhere. Continuously. It never stops. Try this: try and stop your consciousness, try and STOP being aware of the present moment right now. Try it. There's no off button. Ain't gonna happen. And also notice that this consciousness is always there when you are. And it's even there when you're not. It's more subtle to notice that, but as you go to sleep, if you pay close attention as you do, it's quite noticeable that your consciousness persists. You can notice when you fall asleep the phenomena vanish as "you" do, but they vanish IN CONSCIOUSNESS, and reappear there as you wake up. It's not like there's nothing and then consciousness appears; there's consciousness, and then phenomena appear in it as you wake up. There's no "there" there if consciousness isn't there.

So phenomena are appearing and disappearing in consciousness. This is empirically obvious, just look and see if it's so. What ELSE is there to see. If that's true, then that must be what we are. We ARE that. And if you have more complicated versions of what you are, you can examine those; just use discriminating intelligence. "What do I really think I am? Is this true?" Look for the evidence. And is there any OTHER evidence that ISN'T fitting in to my picture of what I am? Be like a "forensic parapsychologist" and try to sort out what the evidence actually supports.

A forensic scientist might have a bunch of bones, artifacts, weapons, and so on, that they have to try and piece them together like a puzzle, to figure out what was going on in a situation. We're like that. We're born into this world, this situation, with no operator's manual or schematic diagram or anything; we have to figure out for ourselves what's really going on. We're in this unknown situation, we've been given a lot of information and misinformation; but we have the evidence of our being, our experience; we may have leaped to conclusions at one point or another in our lives about what is happening here, but if we back up and reassess on the basis of the evidence, skeptically and with discrimination, we may be able to sort it out, separate the wheat from the chaff.

We may have leaped to conclusions at some point, that "Oh, I'm a human being living in a material world, and there're various things I need to do if I want to achieve happiness" and so on, but we can back up from that. We can say "Ok, I jumped to that conclusion at one point in my life. But is it REALLY true? Let me reexamine the evidence. The evidence is all still here; the initial conditions from which I originally drew those conclusions, consciousness, is still here. The body is still appearing, all these things are still here. Let me reexamine that, and see if there are any clearer ways I can piece all this evidence together, and maybe arrive at a more accurate picture of what's going on;

I don't necessarily have to be stuck with my old unexamined conclusions, just because I've been living with them for all these years."

And we may find that some of our root assumptions that have gone into building our stories about what our situation is, are erroneous or arbitrary, and just won't hold water as certainties. There might be OTHER possible interpretations that bear looking into. That's the point - to investigate for yourself. The point is for us to not just take things for granted, because we may have been sold a bill of goods; by our own ignorance, as well as by the ignorance of those around us; by interpreting accidental events in our lives as if they meant something, when they may not have in the sense we have taken them to.

-But some people seem to be pretty thoroughly lost, without any interest whatsoever in trying to find the truth...

Sure, someone might be born with an IQ of 20, and people are born with severe brain damage. Nature produces all these varied lifeforms in different functional condition, but what context can we possibly assess that in? We can't know anything, because we don't know the ACTUAL context of anything, since ultimately the context of reality is infinite and unknowable. So it's speculation to say that "life is the spiritual path" and so on. But for those of us who find ourselves able and on the point of questioning these kind of things, this inquiry becomes an interesting and potentially valuable possibility.

-But we can have quite a meaningful connection to retarded people, and severely damaged people...

EVERYTHING WHATSOEVER is nothing but pure consciousness and pure intelligence; that's what it's all actually made of. EVERY atom, every photon, every quark, every hair on our heads IS the pure, open, totally functional consciousness of the Divine. WE are. Everything is. A junkie alcoholic child molester that's living under a bridge is pure intelligence, pure divine being. EVERYONE is, every THING is. That's the only meaningful context to assess truth in, you know, because that's what everything is made of, that's what everything actually IS. And to look at it in terms of judging any of it with regard to our ideas of success or failure, of relative values, is puerile; because what can be our yardstick for success and failure? By what standard can we say success happens from the viewpoint of reality ?

Well, we say "success is if you're rich, success is if you're healthy, success is if you're a good person, blah blah blah". Says who??? The universe obviously thinks otherwise. The universe makes what it makes, as it makes it; OBVIOUSLY it wants things to be exactly what they are. Warts and all. So who are we to say that warts are undesirable? We can SAY it all we want, but again forensically as a scientist we have to ask, "Is that true?" The universe shows up in all these ways, and the universe IS reality itself, so maybe it's our YARDSTICK for assessing things that's a little off, rather than the universe that's a little off.

-It's interesting that we seem to be addicted to focussing down, but not usually addicted to opening our view...

Well yeah, we call letting our focus open into space "spacing out", and it's usually ridiculed; as we say as a criticism "Oh, so-and-so's spacing out!", as if they're losing it, they're not functioning well. Whereas ACTUALLY that's opening to the fullness of our experience, which IS spacing out or losing the personal identity, and you're a pariah if you do that in society. You're supposed to maintain your personal identity, you're supposed to have "attitude", supposed to have a strong ego that you put forward in order to be socially successful. But the idea of just forgetting who you are and just opening, that's considered if not evil, definitely insane. Because you must be CRAZY to want to do that, people think "Where's the payoff?"

-When I was a kid I tended to be really spaced out...

Calling someone spaced out or calling them a space case or something is a mild insult, you know. It's putting them down. It's saying, "They don't care about anything", which is popularly considered stupid. But that's according to the paradigm of this "cult of individuality" which seems to be the dominant paradigm in modern society, which says you've got to BE somebody, you've got to get ahead, you've got to impress people to succeed, you've got to get ahead of the other guy; which is the whole game structure of ego.

-Then opening to the "big picture" would defuse the impetus to struggle and war, and so on.

Yes. You're opening to the continuity, to the oneness. When you narrow down your focus, you're focussing on perceived differences. "This is different from that, this is better than that, so let's have a war to try to take it." But when you open to the FIELD, you find that everything belongs to this system of wholeness, everything is one with it, everything is an expression of this one thing; it's inherently integrated, it's inherently non-differentiated, so OF COURSE it is peaceful, it's inclusive, it's both/and rather than either/or.

And of course it's the same in our experience personally; when we open to the "noise" in experience instead of just the thoughts, the thoughts are about "this and that", divided, but the noise bridges the thoughts. All these thoughts are discrete aspects of the noise which is inherently inclusive and non-discrete. The noise is a field of vibration, and everything's there, all the possibilities are there. It's not just "this verses that" like we're used to thinking, it's everything in between too; all the maybes, all the could be's and might be's and all the what if's are all there, floating around nebulously and implicitly.

And when we open to those, all of a sudden our train of thought can become a lot less linear, can become a lot less divisive, a lot less either/or, and we can get into a both/and inclusive mode of thought, which is functionally a lot more like the way reality really is. Reality is obviously inclusive, it includes everything that is. And then, we can see THAT. We can see that we ARE that. And at that point WE are inclusive. We are full. We are infinite. And as partiality apparently manifests around us, we can laugh because we know that it's just aspects of fullness.

-So reality is this and that and everything in between.

Of course. Reality is inclusive.

-Which includes the consciousness, that is always looking to see itself...

Yes. The only experiencer here is God. And the only thing experienced here is God. There is nothing else. Seeing reality is seeing that fact. And knowing it intimately, knowing it with certainty to be true, directly, is enlightenment. And it's not hard to do, it only seems hard because it's been painted to us in capital letters as "GOD", capital G, and "ENLIGHTENMENT", capital E... Then we think "Oh my God, a little monkey like me can't possibly approach that, I grovel before it, maybe in thirty billion lifetimes if I'm really good I'll be worthy to even think about it."

But that's more storytelling. God IS great. God is EVERYTHING. God is also LITTLE. God is the dust under our feet. God is our shit. You know, God is the air we breathe; God is the light, God is the substance that reality is made of. God is consciousness. And WE are manifestly consciousness; therefore we are God inherently. If you look and see what you really are, you'll see that whenever YOU are there, consciousness is there. So why bother to draw a distinction; why bother to say that there's me, and there's this little consciousness that I carry around in my head. It's actually the other way around, my head is in consciousness, not consciousness in my head.

We ARE consciousness, and it's quite observable that that's the case if you look and see.

-It gives a new perspective on the first commandment, "Thou shall have no false gods". Our identity as a partial being is a false god. We're worshipping ourselves.

Yes, YES. And if we can manage to see for ourselves, directly, what we TRULY are, that we ARE consciousness, that we ARE god, that's the end of the search, that's the solution to the puzzle, that's enlightenment itself. Your cup runneth over. What else is worth looking for?

-I went to a Santana concert, and every time I looked up, he was moving in the same way that I was moving at the time. I felt like we were coming from the same consciousness...

There's nothing BUT consciousness moving at the same time and in the same direction, always. EVERYTHING is that. Even if it looks different, it's still that. Everything. Everything is always in the perfect harmony and the perfect synchronicity of the hyperintelligent consciousness. God is pure intelligence, and everything is made of that. So everything is functioning with inconceivable intelligence, and inconceivable harmony.

This is so even though every point in space seems to be in a different state from every other point in space. What's happening there is not what's happening here, or here, or here (pointing), and so on. BUT, it's ALL the same pure intelligence. And all of that difference is in total harmony with itself, because it's all the production of just one thing; and it's all made of one thing, and it's all experienced by one thing.

What is experiencing your experience right now is what always experiences everything. It's inviolable, it can't be broken or damaged. The Tibetans call it Dorje, which means diamond; referring to it as the hardest, most impervious, precious thing they knew. Disharmony is a fantasy, it's inconceivable, it can't exist, as everything whatsoever boils down to being nothing other than this one, perfect, transcendental essence, and how can THAT be actually out of harmony with itself?

-So we need to take care of our bodies, because they are the vessels of Spirit?

No, we don't have to take care of it because it's taking care of itself. When you get hungry, you don't DECIDE you're going to get hungry; hunger just spontaneously shows up. And that hunger serves as a motive force to make you go out and try to find some food. IT'LL push you, IT'S doing the work. The hunger is the natural inherent expression of your body taking care of itself by motivating getting food. So it's taking care of itself. And when the hunger arises, it will demand attention, and you'll give it attention, because you are not separate from it.

And your body is NOT the vessel of "your spirit". Everything whatsoever, including "your body", is divine energy spontaneously appearing in divine consciousness. "Spirit" is not IN your body; your body is IN, and wholly MADE OF, "spirit", if we're using the word spirit to mean God, reality. And this "spirit" is not YOURS, what you call you IS nothing other than IT. You ARE THAT, and so are all of its expressions as the forms in consciousness.

-And at that point discernment arises and I decide between a hamburger and health food...

Exactly; but at some point you might want to have a hamburger, it might be what you need. It's not like hamburgers are evil and health food is good; they're both differing modes of the functioning of the universe. The universe produces both hamburgers and health food, so they're both of course divine aspects of reality, interacting with all other aspects in accordance with the inherent patterning of reality. And that patterning is what moves you to choose one or the other; it's all the doing of the inherent nature of things. The flow of events takes care of itself. But you don't need to worry about having preferences in the flow of events, they ARE the flow, too, spontaneously manifesting itself. The universe does everything; "we" are just along for the ride, so to speak.

-This body is going down. May as well face it now, there's no escaping it...

Yeah! But it's irrelevant. It doesn't matter to you, because it's NOT YOU! It's just this unfathomable energy that you're experiencing. But we tend to forget that, we don't realize it as it is...

When we're children we know this. We KNOW we're not our bodies. Every child knows that, that they are the experiencer of everything. And that's defined as an infantile psychological state, a displacement of identity. But that's all ass-backwards. Actually that child IS experiencing reality as it is; but eventually they get hypnotized into thinking they're their body and they start identifying with this body, and then the suffering really starts. Because all of a sudden then things and situations seem to really matter.

Consciousness is a very interesting thing... (laughter) Look at it. Spend more time with your consciousness.

-Do you ever ask "why", with all the problems, violence and chaos of our world situation?

Oh, no. That's just the way it manifests. It IS chaos inherently, from a human perspective. There IS no coherence. Those terms just don't apply. There IS no order in human terms, so there is no chaos relative to it. There is no peace so there is no war relative to the peace. Reality is like lying under a waterfall looking up at the cascades of water pouring down on you. Is it order? Is it chaos? Is it war? Is it peace? Those terms just don't apply; what it actually IS is a nonstop, never repeating cascade of energies JUST AS THEY HAPPEN TO BE, in consciousness.

When we dream, we experience all sorts of apparent things; beautiful, horrific, strange, simplistic, problematic, boring. Is the fact that we experience any of them a PROBLEM? They are apparitions apparently meaningful to the consciousness that dreams them, but according to our normal "human" values, they can be chaotic, negative, and unfathomable. It is exactly the same with the apparent situations we experience in our waking experience; who are WE to say what is "right" and "wrong"? Apparently all these phenomena are an inherent part of the being of reality, or they wouldn't BE!

-I heard that the guy that was responsible for all those junk bonds did more to stimulate the economy than most legitimate business...

Of course. You can argue that Hitler did an awful lot for world peace, because of the repercussions of World War II. You know? But EVERYTHING is embedded in the causal stream, if you want to think in those terms, and as such, any event leads to the ENTIRE future in unpredictable ways, and if any event were different than it is, the entire future would be different.

So what do you do with that? Where does that leave you? It implies a different world view than a simplistic "do-good-actions-if-you-want-good-results" philosophy will give us. It implies a world view of inclusiveness, it implies a world view of forgiveness and acceptance; it implies a world view of harmony, of accepting the harmony of events and things as they are. All circumstances are the expression of BEING, are the expression of the whole universe. And as such all circumstances whatsoever are a CELEBRATION of that being, that universe. We may as well say it's God, we may as well say it's the divine, because there's nothing BUT it.

-In that there's no failure...

Of COURSE there's no failure. Or success. It's all just beauty. Or ugliness if you prefer, doesn't matter. Or the ecstasy of energy cascading through consciousness. But the point is to be with what it IS, rather than trying to capture it with labels. THAT'S our downfall; we keep trying to capture things with labels, saying "It's THIS!". And as soon as you say "It's this", then what about "that"? It's ALL, it's being, it's what we are. It's the flow of events, the flow of experience.

-I knew you were going to say that. (laughter) But there is a striking amount of continuity and similarities of experiences when I'm awake; this room is the same size it always is...

A miss is as good as a mile. The whole idea that this room is the same size as you remember it is a complete fallacy. If you move your head, or shift in your seat, the apparent size of this room and everything in it shifts into entirely new perspectives you've never experienced exactly before, and never will again. When you stand up it's a different size, when you look into it from the hall when you're walking into it it's a different size; which of these sizes is its ACTUAL size?

And every time you have an experience of "this room" it's different from any other time you've ever had, or will have, an experience of it. Which one of these particular experiences is "the room"?

-But if we all took a bunch of tape measures and measured the room, they would all come out the same.

But we'd be using tape measures that expand and contract as you move around... (laughter) How long is a foot, for example? This is a foot (holds hands apart near face), and this is a foot (holds hands farther away from face); go stand three miles away and I'll hold up a foot. Which one is a foot? And you can never experience a foot the same size twice because you'll never be exactly the same distance from the ruler.

From another angle, even if you had incredibly precise laser measuring equipment, the room would never measure exactly the same size twice, because the exact parameters of the measuring couldn't be exactly repeated.

You couldn't measure from the exact same spot to the other exact same spot twice; the atoms in the wall are moving, the atoms and photons in the measuring device are moving, so there's an inherent inexactitude in the repeatability of ANYTHING. So, on two subsequent, necessarily different, experiences of the "same thing", which one is the "real" thing?

-I like your analogy of the ripples in a pond - you set something into motion, and you have good intentions, but you can't know ALL the effects that will follow on your actions-

Of course. Say you're walking by a stream and see an innocent child who's drowning, so you run in and save its life. But that child might turn out to be the great grandfather of a horrible tyrant who's going to cause the deaths and torture of millions of people. How can you know?

-So do you suggest we shouldn't save the child?

No, not at all. I'm suggesting that whether or not you save the child has more to do with how the energy of reality that is appearing as YOU is functioning at the moment you pass the stream, than with whether or not there's an objective situation that you can know anything about. In other words, you WILL do what you WOULD do in those circumstances, including whatever stories you're telling yourself about why you're doing it. And what you WOULD do is subject to constant revision as the energy flow that constitutes your being constantly develops from one moment to the next.

-What's communion with another being?

Every atom is communing with every other atom in the universe all the time. Call it gravity, call it electromagnetic quantum exchange, call it love. Everything is constantly "talking to" everything else in a state of absolute openness and harmony. That's the fact. And if we're not seeing that, we're not seeing the facts, we're seeing confusion, we're seeing falsehood, we're seeing partiality.

-So are we living in a state of resistance, is that why we're not seeing it that way?

Sure, possibly. You can look at it as resistance, you can look at it as attachment to partial views. It's like being addicted; if I'm addicted to something, I get a feedback loop where I'm stuck being obsessed with what I'm addicted to, and I more or less ignore the bigger picture. So we narrow down our game structure, narrow down our field of interest in the universe unnecessarily. We think it's necessary, we have a powerful investment in doing it, for whatever reason. You could look at it as a resistance to the greater, or you could look at it as an obsession with the smaller. But in any case it's emphasizing partiality, instead of being open to the fullness of what actually IS. Be here now; look into what IS here, ALL of it, now.

- How about science? I'm wary of "soft mind", maybe I've been hanging out with new ager's too long...

Well, rightfully so, that stuff is scary. (Laughter) "New Age" thinking is as sloppy as any sloppy thinking. Let me try to explain it from the materialist scientist's point of view.

Suppose the materialist hypothesis is correct. Consciousness is the result of chance juxtapositions of atoms in the brain. So therefore, consciousness must be inherent in those atoms, even if latent. It can't be a new thing that just appears under certain conditions; it must be part of what atoms ARE, even if it requires certain conditions for its expression.

So even if the atoms of our brains fall apart, the seeds of our consciousness are inherent in the matter that they are. So consciousness is inherent in matter; and since we ARE consciousness, and the universe is matter, we are the universe. We are one with what matter and energy IS.

So you get to the same understanding whether you start from consciousness as the base of being, or matter/energy as the base of being. Ultimately we are inseparable from, and nothing but expressions of, the being that the universe is. There's a mind-boggling degree of intelligence in the structure of things; it's obvious that it's inherent in the structure of things. IF it's "all just matter", then matter is INCREDIBLY intelligent. Matter has the inherent property to organize itself into all this. So it boils down to the same thing, no matter how you get to it.

-Looking at some of the amazing experiences people have had, it's laughable at the limited explanations that hard science comes up with...

The problem with "hard" science is that until it has explained EVERYTHING, it hasn't explained anything, because the new idea just around the corner may turn EVERYTHING currently thought upside down and inside out. And any theory of hard science that doesn't include consciousness as one of its central features, is obviously deficient in terms of describing reality; because the cardinal fact of reality as we experience it obviously IS consciousness, and all "scientific" data occur WITHIN consciousness. So that HAS to be taken into account; all phenomena happen in consciousness. Since that's the fundamental fact, any theory that doesn't start from that fact, or at least include that fact, can't model reality accurately.

- Science is working on a unified field theory to explain everything, an equation that describes reality - is that possible?

In a fractal sense, every experience is an encapsulated version of the whole. Like a hologram; if you take a hologram and you cut it into pieces, each piece will contain the entire hologram. Exactly like that, every so-called limited thing actually contains and reflects the unlimited whole; it's the net of Indra. So the equation of reality can be found in anything, anywhere.

But the catch is, you have to have an understanding of the nature of reality to read it. But the equation of reality is simple. Just look at anything, and you're seeing it and nothing but; you have energy in consciousness, and the interwoven relationship of the two is plain to see.

Anything whatsoever is an expression of the equation of the universe; anything whatsoever is a yantra of the whole. (A yantra is a schematic diagram illustrating the interrelationships of realities.) Every atom is a reflection of all aspects of the whole universe, the whole of reality.

-So, HOW does any point refer to the whole?

Any point, any aspect whatsoever of reality, is an embodiment of the whole of reality, because reality isn't made of discrete pieces. Reality is more a function than a thing, and the entirety of it is happening all the time. So if I look at a piece of dust, that's reality happening. If I'm a thousand miles above the Earth and I look at all the civilizations spread out through a super telescope, that's not any more or less complex than me looking at a speck of dust; because they're both instances of the same "system" of reality happening, and the entirety of reality must be functioning for either experience to occur.

Reality can look very complex or it can look very simple, but both of those are untrue, because it's neither simple nor complex; it is always and in all aspects completely, fully, what it is.

-In science, there're so many levels, deeper than the atomic levels and so on...

There ARE no levels actually; it's like a fractal. There are different layers of focus, but each layer of focus is just a view of the whole from that perspective, and there's an infinite number of possible perspectives. So it's not actually "deeper", it's just different. We think of it as deeper because we think of bigger and smaller, but those are arbitrary differentiations.

-How can we know that the entire universe that we know isn't in a speck of dust?

Right. There's no absolute perspective, any point of view is as central, as "middle", as any other. There's no hierarchy of size in actuality, because for those ideas to be meaningful there would have to be an end, an absolute maximum largeness or smallness to use as a reference point, and there just ISN'T. So no matter where your point of view seems to be, it's always right in the middle. Go a little "smaller", and then THAT'S the middle. Go larger, the same thing. You're always right in the center of the fullness of being; it just always looks different as you shift your perspective.

So any aspect of reality is actually the entirety of reality, because there's no actual reference point that can be established as "bigger" or "more complete", just a different view of the same thing. This is what is meant by "emptiness" in Buddhism; ANY instance of reality is as big, as small, as real, or as unreal as any other instance of reality, no matter how much bigger or smaller or more central the other instance seems to be.

So all points of view are actually referenceless, they have no reference points from which any meaningful assessments can be made about them whatsoever; so ultimately you can't say anything final about them. Without a fixed reference point from which to assess anything, anything we say about it is arbitrary. As we cannot know finally what anything actually IS in any sense, all our so-called "knowledge" about things is "fuzzy" and arbitrary, and easily subject to challenge by another, necessarily equally "fuzzy" point of view. "Emptiness" doesn't mean that things don't exist, it means that they're ABSOLUTELY indeterminate; we can't pin them down, we can't say anything about them which isn't arbitrary. What things are is ABSOLUTELY open-ended.

-What about prayer?

This IS the prayer. This is the prayer right here. Just BEING is its own prayer. We're all already blessed. Everything that is is blessed, is the divine.

-Can prayer help someone be effective?

Maybe prayer can help heal someone, or maybe they would have gotten better anyway. Maybe the prayer that just healed someone, killed someone else. Who can say? Because everything is a part of and effects everything else already, it's impossible to separate out what any event has effected and what it hasn't, and what the "results" are, or to assess them as positive or negative. The universe is too complex, too nonlinear to be able to know.

-Like you say, we pray for a clean atmosphere, but somewhere there's a species that is praying for more hydrocarbons, because that's what makes them thrive...

Of course. Because when we poison our environment so that we go extinct, whatever species becomes the next dominant species, and can thrive under those new conditions, will see us as their benefactors. There was a time apparently in Earth's history when the dominant gas in the atmosphere was carbon dioxide, and oxygen was a poison and a pollutant to the bacteria that were dominant then. But there was a strain of bacteria that excreted oxygen, poisoning their atmosphere. But they were OUR benefactors, giving us the oxygen WE need.

We may have a nuclear war and completely poison the environment, and cockroaches or something are going to come along and go, "Thank you! Praise God for providing us with what we need!" And then THEY'LL trash the environment for themselves, but create conditions that are great for another life form, and so on. The cycle just keeps going forever.

-And that's why you say "unless you know everything, you don't know anything"...

Yes.

-You're in a relationship with someone and you think they're telling the truth and it turns out they're lying to you...

Look at it this way. Anything's sole responsibility is to be what it is. You caring about truthfulness is you being who you are. That other person lying is them being who they are. It's a cat's job to hunt, torture and kill birds. It's the birds job to try and get away. Why? Because cats are cats and birds are birds. Why is that? Will of God. The nature of the universe. Why is it your job to care and why is it someone else's job to lie to you? Because you are you and they are them. WHO did it?

-But to perpetrate something on somebody else...

It's your job to feel like that, so you are being true to yourself and expressing what you are. How could you do otherwise? If you go around with wild abandon hurting people perhaps that wouldn't be you, at this moment. And if it WAS you then that's what you WOULD do. You would be being true to yourself.

-I wonder about accountability. It's an anarchistic...

No, it's not anarchistic at all. It's the unfoldment of an incredibly intelligent highly structured system. Whose responsible for the great earthquake of 1906? Who did it? All those houses burned all those people killed. Who did it?

-Acts of nature are different.

YOU'RE not an act of nature? What made you? The same thing that made you is the same thing that made the 1906 earthquake, my dear.

-Yes, but I also have the ability to stop and say "This is going to affect another person"...

You have the ability, but do you have the motivation? And if you DO, what put the motivation there?

-I have no idea.

And if you don't have the motivation, what DIDN'T put the motivation there? And if the motivation IS there, how can you remove it? If the motivation was not there, how could you instill it? Think about it. How can anything be anything other than what the universe makes it to be? Look at the unutterable perfection, that everything IS just exactly what it is. How could it be more perfect? It's a done deal. It's all over. It's an infinitely complex puzzle assembling and simultaneously dismantling itself with INCONCEIVABLE precision. We're just watching it all unfold. You're being you, I'm being me, the floor's being the floor, the republicans are being the republicans, the plate tectonics are being the plate tectonics. It's all this just incredible, elaborate, intelligent system that is spontaneously unfolding itself. It's a done deal. It's beautiful. It's exquisite. It's well called the "Great Perfection".

-So where's the responsibility in all that? Who's to blame?

There's no responsibility, because there's no separable entity to TAKE responsibility, because every entity is a creation of the whole system. Everything boils down to the whole system itself. There's no separable entity. You can't draw a line and say "I'm here, and I stop HERE and THERE the universe takes over. The universe makes a lump which is the island which I think of as "me", which then goes off and interacts with the rest of the universe which is "it". It's a circle. It's a snake eating its tail.

The universe makes itself through all of its pieces in real time, so the pieces aren't really pieces. They're the orifices of the universe making itself, interacting. Every atom is the orifice of the universe making itself, interacting with all other atoms in real time, which is the universe creating itself. And the UNIVERSE is doing it all. The atoms are not responsible. They're being done, the universe is doing them. The universe is doing everything. Every quark in this room is a search light from God.

-I don't know how to deal with the innocent children and animals that get tortured.

What do you mean by deal with it?

-I guess I keep trying to find a place where it makes sense to me.

What does "make sense" mean?

-(Laughing) I guess like there's a little box I can put it in. I try to think "Oh it's their karma and what they chose to do this life..."

Is any of that true?

-It's true and it's not true at the same time. It's a story...

Okay, good. The fact is, it seems to happen, okay? Why does it happen?

-...because there are a lot of angry tortured souls on the planet...

And why are there a lot of angry tortured souls on the planet?

-Their upbringing and experience?

Why do they have that kind of upbringing and experience?

-Because they were at the mercy of who ever was bringing them up...

And why would THOSE people be like they were?

-Well, like you say, I guess the causes keep going back in history, ultimately because of the big bang?

There's your box. Did you know that among cats that are living in their natural environment, it's very normal for a male to go and kill all of the offspring of another male, so that it can then inseminate the female to have ITS children propagated? Gender biology. Maybe similar mechanisms are at work with human behavior. It's all just workings of nature. You can't extricate ANYTHING from nature. The idea that nature is supposed to conform to our ideas of morality is the most insipid child's fantasy. It MIGHT be wonderful if it was true. But is it? Nature DOES what nature DOES, and there's an incredible intelligence about it. It you find its intelligence on its own basis, you may find a profound and amazing symmetry to it. Whereas if you look at it from a simplistic moralistic human, childish, wishful point of view, you might find it wanting.

But then you're criticizing that intelligence that makes you, that makes EVERYTHING what it is. You're criticizing God, saying "You're not supposed to be like that." Says who? Look into it. Look into the whole thing. Try and take the true perspective as best you can. See the facts of the case as best you can. If you get to the point where you're even LOOKING at it, you're home free. Keep looking, keep sorting it out. And you'll get a clearer and clearer picture of what's going on. It does itself. Consciousness gets to a point where it wants clarity for itself; that's why we're all here. We're in a point in our lives, where it's an important thing to us. To fight for that clarity. The chick chipping its way out of the eggshell of delusion into clarity. When you get to the point where it's time to chip out of that eggshell, you're motivated to do it. At that point it's basically a done deal.

But even THAT, of course, is an expression of the force of nature. The same force that makes the child torturers, makes us here in Satsang doing this. So you can't criticize the one without criticizing the other. If you accept one you have to accept the other. What put Christ on earth also put Hitler on earth. They're parts of the same pattern. And it may be that the pattern is so complex, and you're taking it out of context. There's a context that if you saw the child torturers from, you'd see they were a part of the mosaic of things that's incredibly beautiful and incredibly perfect, and there's a symmetry and a harmony to every aspect of it.

-Do you feel we have free choice?

Well that's a loaded question, isn't it. What do you mean by "We"? What do mean by "free"?

-Is there a destiny? Did God set out a path for each person? Did I choose to come here to Satsang?

You are the kind of person, through no fault of your own, that apparently chose to come to Satsang. Through your inherent nature, your genetic hereditary, the accidents that have happened to you socially along the way, the history of the universe has molded you and shaped you into being the kind of person you are, who is motivated to make the kind of choices you do at the time you make them; so in what sense can your choices be free? So it's just pure consciousness.

Your choices could be free if you could decide not to be Mikaela, but to be someone else entirely. Can you do that? It would be an interesting choice, if you could decide to be Arnold Schwarzenegger or decide to be Hitler or Jesus Christ and then make the choices THEY would make. If you could do THAT, that might be truly free choice, but I would argue that you can't actually make any choices beyond the gamut of what you could make as Mikaela. Which may be a broad range, but none the less, calling them free from that point of view, doesn't really hold water.

And also supposing that there's choice, supposing that there's freedom, supposing that there's an entity, you, that could EXERCISE that freedom, that HAS choices; are all metaphysical assumptions that might not be based in reality. Reality is unknowable, unsayable. What an event IS is unknowable, unsayable. They aren't these superficial, simple, "objective" things we say they are.

So we CAN say "I DECIDE to come to Satsang", but that whole notion is an incredibly simplistic statement. Because reality is this infinite, indescribable, nonlinear, nonmechanical occurring. So in what sense can this simplistic statement be said to meaningfully apply to reality? In other words, reality and every"thing" that occurs in its context is infinitely complex, infinitely subtle, infinitely intangible, infinitely inscrutable, infinitely mysterious, a bottomless pit of unknowability; so in what sense can you say you "decide" to come to Satsang?

I'm not saying that that's not a "true" statement as far as it goes. But it's such an incredibly vast oversimplification of an unknowable reality, that in what sense can it be meaningfully applicable?

The question of whether or not there's free will or predestination... Again, you're dealing with very simplistic models. The onus is on YOU to demonstrate that they're applicable at all to this intangible infinite being that is reality. In my observation, it's impossible to build a meaningful bridge between any model of reality and reality itself. Anything you can say about it, any picture of what's going on, diverges infinitely from reality itself. Because reality is infinitely infinite. Infinitely unknowable, mysterious, miraculous. It exists only in itself. There are NO reference points from which to assess it, or to get any point of view on it at all. It exists inside itself alone. You can't get perspective on reality, no perspective but IT itself. It's all totally self referential and infinite, so what do you do with THAT?

You can say "it's free will or predestination". You can argue that all you want. But again, you're kind of pissing in the wind, because the reality, immediate obvious reality, is ungraspable. So even if you make one of those statements, it's not verifiable. You CAN make a good argument either way. When someone asks that question, more typically I'll give them the opposite answer than they expect, not because it's TRUE, but because it's unsettling. It helps to shake up people's conceptual fixations. The point is that there's NOT some fixed truth that you can find, some actual "way things are" that can be delineated. The point is to let go of the fixed truths that you think there are, that you are clinging on to. When you drop ALL truths, all your beliefs, there's a possibility of seeing Reality. Reality is beyond any frame of reference.

-I'm always trying to find spiritual integration...

There is absolutely NO integration in the phenomena of experience. There's just a free form coming together of things and moving apart of things. Any apparent patterning that we see, the intelligence of our consciousness superimposes on the raw energy of experience.

Egoically we cling to solidity, to try to create some kind of coherence in all this incoherence. Things are constantly falling apart. They were never really together to begin with! It's like particles of dust in a dust storm whirling around, and they seem to form occasional patterns. Then we think "Oh! I see something." But it's all just an accident. It's all just chaos. It's all free form chaos that we have no control over and no relationship to, except that they ARE us, they are appearing in our consciousness, the energy that we are.

Of course this is very contrary to the sort of mundane world view that many people seem to have: "We live in a concrete world and there are all these situations that we need to take care of and deal with and solve. We think we're a concrete thing and we have to fight for our safety, status, and achievement" or whatever.

But in actual fact, all of these patterns that show up in our experience are completely non patterned in any terms we can grasp; completely chaotic, completely accidental, caused by chaotic and accidental influences that are themselves momentary. And the patterns THEMSELVES are constantly changing, drifting and dissipating. So in fact, any kind of integration is a myth. The only true integration can be seeing THIS truth as the state of affairs, and the fact that intelligence itself, consciousness itself, is not in ANY WAY adversely affected, OR beneficially affected by these patterns that seem to be going on in it.

And of course we ourselves ARE that background consciousness, that background intelligence where everything is happening, rather than the specific accidental aspect of a small phenomena APPEARING in it that we may typically identify ourselves with. We think "I'm this body and I'm in this situation and all these things are going on and it's really a problem, because I have to arrange this and I'm really hoping that that happens..." All of that is a fabrication. The FIRST assumption is wrong. I'm NOT this body. What I call the body appears IN Consciousness. But even calling it a body is lumping together a bunch of accidental phenomena as if it was a whole coherent entity.

In actual fact there's just no coherence whatsoever. There're degrees of coherence, it could be argued, but that's just begging the question, because there's no fundamental coherence. Even if some of the patterns are dissipating more slowly than others, doesn't mean that they're anymore substantial, INTEGRATED, or actual than the ones that go fast like clouds or lighting bolts. Those may be more relatively rapid.

The true coherence is the coherence of being itself. But THAT'S not IN the patterns of phenomena. They are just chaotic; there's no sense to be made of them. There is nothing that can be made, and anything that IS made is dissipating instantaneously.

CONCEPTS

-So are you saying that conceptualizing about what IS, is basically pointless?

Of course. It's exactly that; it's pointless. But there's no reason NOT to do it, either. You can have fun; it's play, and might be useful in some regards. But if you BELIEVE it, you've been sold a bill of goods.

Thinking inherently boils down to thinking about abstract, supposedly separate entities, because you can't think about things and conditions unless there are things and conditions to think about! I can think about you, think about me, think about what we're doing, think about what we're going to do, and so on. That presupposes that all those things; you, me, things to do, etc., actually exist as separate entities, if the thinking is to correspond to reality. But if everything is just part of a flow, if all our quantum particles are just co-mingling, if the energies they actually ARE is just this ebb and flow of reality, then how true, how accurate, can all this thinking really be?

Nouns imply separate entities, discretely existing things. Like "person", "floor", "rug", "candy". It presupposes that there is a person that is separable from the floor, and from the rug and the candy. But actually there's only the one mysterious system of being, that shows up as what we name person, floor, rug and candy simultaneously. But the words belie that. The words suggest that there actually ARE separate things.

-We embrace these separate words, like "peace", then have emotional associations with them, thinking they're good or bad, instead of embracing the whole as it actually is...

Yes. Well, the Buddha put it very well; if you start having preferences, start choosing this or rejecting that, you're bound to get frustrated, to suffer dissatisfaction sooner or later. Because the world comes as a whole; we inevitably get the one WITH the other, you can't separate things out. If you want peace, what are you going to do about war? If you want happiness, what are you going to do about sadness? Whereas if you just "go with the flow" so to speak, work with reality as it presents itself, then it's all there, and what's the problem? Because then you're not defining things as being problems.

You can deal with events as they arise in whatever ways seem appropriate because that's part of functioning; but that functioning arises within the whole, just as the various situations arise within the whole. The situations arise within the context of the whole, dealing with them arises within the context of the whole, and the results arise within the context of the whole. And those results lead to future actions, all inseparable from the one flow of events.

And the results of action are ALWAYS more complex than we expect. We try to do something good, and some of its repercussions will be bad. We do something really naughty, and it has some positive repercussions. It's inevitable; because in reality, every event is like a pebble thrown into some water; the ripples spread out in ALL directions, not just in the direction we may wish them to go. So trying to do the "right thing" is an absurdity. I mean, there's nothing wrong with TRYING; but in reality, you have to acknowledge that your action will have countless repercussions, many of which will not be what your intention was to achieve.

-So we should let go of attachment to results...

Well, yeah, or just live with frustration.

-Or disappointment...

Or disappointment. Yeah, there are lots of different words for the same thing.

-I've been thinking about vision tonight, really noticing, what is it? WHERE am I looking when I look at something?

THAT'S just where to look. That's JUST the right thing to do. What is looking? What am I seeing? What is it? What does my experiencing actually consist of?

-And at the same time, it's not to just see that it's "energy in consciousness", it's to see what it actually IS.

See what it is. Yes. Let go of ANY preconceptions. Let go of everything. Christ is supposed to have said, "Unless you become like a little child you won't enter the kingdom of heaven". THIS is what he's talking about. Little children don't KNOW what they're looking at; so they can really SEE it. When we know what we're looking at we don't see it, we only see our preconceptions of it.

-It's really weird, what "things" are when we really see them...

Yes! But you're noticing that, that's the point. To notice; criticize everything. Notice what it IS, and criticize EVERYTHING you've been told about what things are. Criticize your own thoughts about it. Be a scientist; be skeptical. Don't believe anything until you've investigated it for yourself repeatedly.

-...That reminds me of the Bardo teachings, getting caught in a "god realm".

Precisely. Getting caught in ANY apparitions, believing they are "real", are actual, is ultimately a "hell realm"; because this "getting caught" is what hell consists of. Whatever anything IS, we always THINK it looks like a god realm, don't we? When you're a hungry ghost you think "Oh, man, look at that! If I JUST can get that, everything will be fine!" And that attachment IS hell. Whatever it looks like; getting sucked in is hell.

-Sri Yukteswar's in a bardo... he said everyone should try to come to the loka where he reincarnated, according to Yogananda in "Autobiography of a Yogi".

Spiritual teachers are all liars. (laughter) Because more than anyone, they're the ones who KNOW that it's actually impossible to tell the truth as it is. They KNOW they're lying. The rest of us can actually have a sincere belief that we're telling the truth. A genuine spiritual teacher KNOWS for a FACT that he's lying. So if he's a genuine spiritual teacher, he's a liar.

It's all artifice, you know. Trying to give spiritual teachings boils down to manipulation, magic tricks, and artifice.

Because if you're genuine you know that you HAVE to do that, it's the only way to try to communicate the incommunicable; You're playing tricks on people, to try to trick them out from under the tricks they play on themselves, by which they get themselves stuck.

And you do it under the guise of showing them something valuable. Whereas actually you're showing them something of little actual value that will hopefully do the trick in snapping them out of what they're hung up on. Because there isn't actually ANYTHING that's valuable, except Being itself, which can't be communicated. Everything "else" is equally valueless. THAT'S the truth.

-It's like a sleight of hand; "Look over HERE"...

Yeah, it's totally that. It's magic. It's magic tricks.

-I was walking yesterday noticing all the beauty around me, and I thought about naming, the elaborate taxonomy that scientists have whereby they can name everything around us. And we think because we have all those names, we somehow can understand how that leaf came out of nowhere...

Exactly! And all that taxonomy is generalization. Because although you may know the genus etc. of a plant, that doesn't say anything about THAT particular plant. That plant is different from this plant, even if they're the same classification or family. They're different. Everything about them's different. Different genetic structure, different history; they appear different, and they're each even different than THEMSELVES in the next instant, as everything is constantly changing.

-Everything is different from everything else...

There're no reference points, there's no bedrock. There're no... What are those points they use in surveying? There're no benchmarks. And since you don't have a starting point, anyplace that you think you are conceptually is totally arbitrary. You can't say "I know where this is because I know where THAT is, and what its relationship to "this" is".

-So we're back to "if you don't know everything, then you can't know anything".

Yeah. We're babes in the woods.

-I realized that when I was a kid I was given all these erroneous myths about who I was by my family...

Yeah, Garbage in, garbage out. How can we formulate a clear understanding of who and what we are when we're being fed erroneous information about that, at a time when our critical thinking abilities are undeveloped?

-I think it's all identity addiction...

Yes. Identity is our one addiction. Identity's our one problem. The false, partial identity... We get addicted to having this sense of identity, and then we do anything we can to reinforce our game. It's like we believe we're a character in a play, and we just really want to work our way through that play and come out "on top". If we could just drop the whole thing, if we could just say, "I don't care", all of a sudden, this investment in identity just deflates. And THEN we have the openness and the space to see where we are, where we really are. As long as we're obsessed with this identity, obsessed with needing to be a certain thing, we're stuck. It's a tar baby, you can't get out of it.

-So thoughts and desires still arise even as we start to see this, but our relationship to them starts to change...

Well, we're used to thinking of our thoughts and desires as problems, or important aspects of our identity; but when you see the true perspective of what they are, they are energy spontaneously arising and disappearing in consciousness, like everything is. And they also do their dance in harmony with themselves, just like everything does. They don't "mean" anything. What any phenomenon "means", is the being of God and the universal harmony of the divine energy with itself, which all phenomena are produced by and consist of. Every thought we have is the same. When you think a thought... For example I may think I'm going to get a beer, but what I'm really thinking about is the universal harmony of god. I'm just CALLING it "going to get a beer", but THAT'S what that actually IS. "Going to get a beer" is a dumbing down, an oversimplified description, of what it really is, the miraculous arising of the panorama of divine energy in consciousness.

If I go to a bar, what's the bar made of? Divine energy in consciousness; pure energy, pure light. It's a temple; it's the very body of god. What's beer? Beer is pure intelligence, it's pure consciousness, it's vibrating energy in consciousness, just like everything is. So what can anything mean other than that simple fact of what it is? Things mean what they are, and everything is pure light. Everything is pure consciousness/intelligence, existing in consciousness, perceived by consciousness, made of consciousness; end of story.

-I was thinking how much like computers we are. I was educated to be a doctor, and the entire experience of getting that education was like getting a software upgrade...

Sure. You learned the rules for playing an elaborate game. You learned a new program. And society places such stock in our individual status depending on what games we're programed to play. "I'm a doctor, I'm a clerk, I'm a wino"...

That's why we play all these games. We play all these games with the idea that there's some payoff; some status, some reward. That's the concept of what human life is supposed to be that is the dominant paradigm in our society, in our culture. What is someone who's not running a program? What are they?

It gets back to addiction to states. EVERYTHING is part of the same process, the unfolding of the one reality, so nothing has a superior status to something else just because it's in a different point in that process. Butterflies aren't better than caterpillars. Teachers aren't better than students. Nice people aren't better than jerks.

This whole issue of our separate bodies... Our ACTUAL condition is what it IS, indefinable and unknowable; but we superimpose arbitrary definitions and conceptual maps and ideas of what's going on onto that, that aren't necessarily supported by hard evidence. They are leaps to conclusions. We do this all over the place.

Our ACTUAL condition is one of enlightenment, being pure consciousness within which pure energy cascades as experience, as a unique system. Why don't we know it? Simply because we've DEFINED ourselves as unenlightened, and we don't question that. We've defined ourselves as being in bodies. We've defined ourselves as failing and lacking, and as limited, problematic beings. But if you look very closely, each one of those definitions is not supported by the evidence. If you really do it forensically and look very closely at... "Well, I think this, because of this and this, and I think that because of that and that". But what are THEY? What ARE each of the elements in that chain of logic?

When you peel away those layers of the onion of our concepts, sooner or later you say "Why did I think that? Well, it kind of made sense at the time... or my parents told me, or everyone around me was acting as if it was the case, so I guess I thought it was." We were raised in a world where all the bodies around us are behaving as if their consciousness is contained IN them, and so naturally we superimpose that map on ourselves. If you look very closely, there's no evidence for it. Or the evidence is circumstantial at best.

-Descartes; I think, therefore I am. That statement seems to start the separation process, you're identified with your stories, mind.

Actually that statement with its two possible semantic interpretations defines the two possible views of Reality. The more traditional interpretation, that you seem to be talking about, is "My analytical mode of thinking somehow generates this sense of self." On that level, that's where confusion comes from. That's where all the delusions and supposed unenlightenment is generated. On the other hand, if you interpret the "thinking" as cognition, functioning of mentality pure and simple, then it's a true statement; because where there is functioning of MIND, there is BEING. In other words, functioning of mind and Being are identical. Which is true. Mind, as consciousness, is Being. Mind is Being as experience.

-Based on some of his other teachings of the universe as a machine...

That notion of a universe that's mechanistic and has produced us all, again makes perfect sense depending on how you interpret it; because the universe is WHATEVER is. It is a system that is functioning producing everything, and that functioning produces our experience, so in that sense it is all mechanistic. The one fundamental system of causes, whatever those causes may or may not be in themselves, produces everything, and produces us and all phenomenon, and produces the inner workings of them all. Now whether that's mechanistic or not is another issue, and again that's a semantic issue too; because even if there are no "mechanics" as such, then the word mechanics can still refer to the workings of the energies that actually DO produce experience, whether they are or aren't that exactly.

-But I prefer associating with more "spiritually " aware people...

This is an important point; but it's about YOU, where you're at in your evolution, not an absolute value. What seems right for you is a function of what you are at this moment in time. What's nourishing for you and what's NOT nourishing are relative to how you are manifesting right now. But those are relative terms in relation to functionality, in terms of the metabolism of your evolution, and not static values or absolutes. You are investigating for yourself the meaning of what it is to be "spiritual", and exploring different stances in your behavior with regard to that. After you explore these issues thoroughly for yourself, you will discover that spirituality is the very nature of reality, and life itself IS the "spiritual path"; and ALL people are on it, if there were actually any people...

-But then we can do that with every experience, I like this and don't like that...

Yes. But the problem isn't having the judgments, the judgments are a matter of practicality, of the functioning of your life. But the context within which you view the things... Just because something seems to mean something particular in your life at the moment, doesn't mean that THAT'S what it IS in itself. And you can hold both of those. You can say, "At this point in my evolution this is toxic for me and I will try to avoid it; BUT I can see that it isn't inherently toxic, it's a natural aspect of the functioning of the universe and at other points in my evolution it may actually become nourishing and valuable to me."
Everything constantly changes. We need different energies at different times.

-The way we use words confuses this so much; we should try to use language more precisely.

But it's IMPOSSIBLE to use language rightly. Because there's only one true word: "being". So if I use a sentence that has any word other than "being" in it, I'm lying, I'm speaking inaccurately. Pure and simple. But if we realize what words ACTUALLY mean, which is that they each refer to the totality of being as it is, they are synonyms of being, then you can use words with wild abandon, and you're still telling the truth.

I use words like an art form. I know I'm lying superficially. But I use the lies as tricks to try to seduce people into shifting their awareness into seeing reality from different points of view than they've become locked into by their beliefs. So I'm quite aware that I'm lying; but when you see reality as it is, you can see its inexpressibility; and you let go of trying to express it with precision, and embrace expressing it with allusion.

-I guess it's important to try to be truthful and not lie...

All that is predicated on the idea that there is a truth that CAN be told, and that there are lies that can be told. The truth is as much a lie as a lie is a lie, verbally. Since the ACTUAL true nature of being CAN'T be told as it is, ANY words are basically lies; so what difference does it make what you say? Both our words and our motivations for saying them, are themselves uncontrollable spontaneous expressions of universal being, after all...

The important thing as always is to SEE the reality of being as it actually is, which we always ARE. To see what IS, AS IT IS, as best we can, nakedly; because THAT ALONE is the Truth. EVERYTHING else is a lie. Being equals truth. Being equals our identity, what we are. That's what being self realized is, directly seeing the truth of THAT. Self knowledge. Seeing being as it is, which is seeing MYSELF as I am; which could be called seeing consciousness as it is. Seeing awareness as it is. Seeing God as it is. Realizing God. Realizing Reality. That's the only place where true spirituality really exists, and where the idea of "truth" has any validity at all.

-So you can lie all you want.

Well, you're going to lie anyway, it's inevitable. When we choose what to say and what not to say, that inherently creates a lie, since the true state of things is inclusive. All our subtle verbal spin-doctoring motivated by our investment in our ego is lies, even "trying" to be truthful is nothing other than that; so until we have no ego motivation WHATEVER we will be nothing but liars. And even after that...?

And the lying isn't even lying really, it's all just an unfoldment of energy too. The universe evolves for us to be thinking human beings, so we fabricate all this stuff, then toss it around and negotiate it in all of our personal politics. WE didn't do it. WE'RE not guilty. The UNIVERSE is doing it. So it's all a part of reality itself. The lying is as much an expression of IT as trying to be truthful. Reality "wants" it to be there or it wouldn't be there. But again by the same token, it isn't REALLY there! Because what it IS, is nothing whatever other than Reality being as it is. Naming it "truthfulness" or "lying" is just a conceptual map that we overlay on this spontaneous BEING. What a tangled web we weave...

-It's kind of like when we were kids pretending...

That's what we do as adults, only we've forgotten that we're pretending. It's ALL pretense. "You're a Republican or a Democrat." "Are you for the Giants or are you for the

Yankees?" Neither, I'm me, I AM. All this gamesmanship is all pretense, but we generally forget that we're pretending, attribute reality to it. We attribute reality to all the entities that we've defined into existence, including ourselves and each other, different systems we think are so called objective realities. But they are all DEFINED into existence, conceptually. They're all a pretense that we've forgotten Is a pretense, all nothing but imagination.

In my opinion, 95% of Buddhist teachings are bullshit, are pretty humanistic wish fulfillment fantasies. The "historical" Buddha didn't teach most Buddhist teachings. Buddha apparently taught the four noble truths, the first three of which are as true as anything that can be spoken:

1) That human life is inherently frustrating.

2) That frustration is caused by attachment and aversion, by wanting things to be different than one thinks them to be; by wanting supposed conditions and by not wanting other conditions.

3) That with the cessation of attachment and aversion you get the cessation of frustration. In other words, when you stop needing things to be one way or another, when you stop wanting the peace and not wanting the child torturer, you get a cessation of frustration, cessation of sorrow.

4) The "eight fold path", tricks intended to effect truth #3.

The other basic tenet of Buddhism, realization of which takes care of "Noble Truths" one through three in one fell swoop and removes the need for four, is "There are no entities", which I go into in great detail with you all. Once you see the truth of this fact, you see conclusively that there is nothing whatever to HAVE attachment to or aversion from, and no one to have it; problem solved. And you see that this is the inherent condition of things that has always obtained.

That's Buddhism for you. All the rest, the mindfulness, compassion and loving kindness is an addition later on that was included for crowd control and politics. If there are no entities, the MOST basic tenet of Buddhism, then WHO is supposed to have compassion, and for WHOM? If you get the essence of the teaching, all the details become moot.

Christianity is the same deal. Christ would roll over in his grave, if he had a grave, if he saw what modern Christianity was. Modern Christianity bears no relationship to the original teaching of Christ. The same with Buddhism. Most spirituality, most spiritual teachings, especially the formulaic ones, boil down to wish fulfillment and public crowd control.

Look at Christianity. Modern Christian teachings were decided politically 300 years after his death. It was decided what the official gospels were and what was going to be denied out of politically expedient reasons; decided by the people in power, for their own agenda, to maintain their power. Look at the history of the Vatican. We're talking politics here. Christ was not talking politics, Christ was talking liberation. Christ was talking God. You can use the promise of God to enslave people, as religious leaders and politicians have discovered time and again.

All models are false, you can't model Reality. They may be useful, but they're fingers pointing to the moon. They're useful if you want to try to talk about IT, to try to indicate IT, but they are NOT themselves true; because the actual mechanism of Reality CANNOT be described. It can be pointed to, but not definitively delineated.

But we've all been seduced by lies; been seduced by stories that we're separate independent beings, that we're incomplete, that we're not good, or certainly not perfect. That if we only do "such and such" then we'll be better and things will be ok. This is the constant pattern that is continuously reflected in society's "consensus reality". It's ubiquitous, implicit in advertising and media, the way we're raised, the mindsets of the people who raised us. All this cultural information that we encounter as children, it's all permeated with this idea of being "separate" , "incomplete", "lacking", "inadequate"; and if you only do something, if you only succeed, if you only make money, if you only find love, if you're only "spiritual" enough in some particular way, if you only can become beautiful, if you're only smart enough, if you're only ANYTHING, fill in the blank, then it'll all be somehow remedied.

There are equally perverse negative fixations, too. Some people think "if I only lose enough, suffer enough pain, deprive myself enough"; all these psychological fixations are expressions of the same theme: that we are lacking, that we are incomplete. But... is it true? Look for yourself, is it true?

But we can't access the experience of our inherent completeness until we can SEE that completeness, and see that it's inherent in what we ARE, and what being itself is. In reality we can't POSSIBLY lose it, so we don't need to find it or cling to it. Then, all of a sudden, it's like money in the bank. You don't need to go anywhere to get what you already have. You know, you can just swim around in it, like Scrooge McDuck in his money vault.

-The word "define" comes from "de-finis", to find an end to.

You can't find an "end" to anything. In experience you can't find an end; there're no edges, no borders, no boundaries to ANY aspect of experience, of reality. Since there're no ends, no boundaries, no fixed reference points, where do you start from? Where do you end up? All systems of human thought boil down to having arbitrary fixed points that are defined into existence, and then the whole system of thought, a whole metaphysic, is developed from there. But if you look closely, there ARE NO FIXED POINTS in the actuality of our experience, so these systems are entirely arbitrary. Everything collapses. And what it collapses to is the reality of experience BEING AS IT IS, which is ultimately beyond analysis. It's self-evident, TOTALLY obvious, but we can't SAY what it IS.

-So with this understanding, where does disease fit in?

Disease is an arbitrary designation of experience. It's part of the process of events just like everything is part of the process of events. Healing is part of the process of events, disease is part of the process, happiness is part of the process, sorrow is part of the process; and from what perspective can we say one's good and one's bad? The one leads to the other, so if the one's good then the other must be good too, because it leads to it, it's part of the same flow of reality.

War leads to peace. Peace leads to war. Which one do you like? If you like peace you're saying "I like what leads to war". If you like war you're saying "I like what leads to peace"; because YOU CAN'T SEPARATE OUT PIECES OF THE SYSTEM. It's a flow, it's a continuum. So as soon as you pick one piece and say "Yeah! This is it, I like THIS one", you're creating a lie, because that one piece necessarily includes all the other pieces by implication.

And not just by implication in an abstract intellectual sense, by implication in terms of cause and effect. They coexist; they co-create each other. You know, disease co-creates health; health co-creates disease. Because the system of reality is an indivisible, organic whole. And from our little bitty human perspective, who are WE to say what's good or bad?

Maybe there's a scheme of things in which disease is a vital part of our metabolism, it actually helps our evolution.

And that actually is my experience, because every time I've had a serious illness I've emerged from it evolved a quantum level up from where I was before the disease. So it may be that disease is just a kind of experiential chrysalis that we find ourselves enfolded in when we're becoming the butterfly of the next step in our unfoldment. Who knows? But at any rate, we certainly can't say for sure what it is, because whatever it is is infinite and open-ended, like everything is, and so it's fundamentally a mystery.

-Then would you allow disease without doing anything about it?

Allow it or fight it, because fighting disease is ALSO a part of the infinite, open-ended reality process, too. But everything we do; everything we allow; everything we strive for, everything we fight against; all of those things are all inextricably part of the same flow, of the same system that reality is. So there's no reason to differentiate any of them out, or to single any of them out as being good or bad, or a problem or a solution, because we CAN'T know.

Because the one thing leads to and includes all the other things ultimately.

So fighting disease ultimately perpetuates disease as well as healing disease. They're each part of the system that makes disease, and part of that same system that heals disease. Life and death are in the same inextricable relationship. So why bother to single them out? I mean, part of the problem is semantic; the way we use language, we have all these separate words, so we think there must be separate things.

We have disease, we have health, we have war, we have peace; we have success, we have failure. And the semantic logic implies that if we have all these separate words, there must be actual separate conditions that they indicate, right? So we come to think we live in a world that's sliced and diced into all these separate conditions, objects, and actions; but the reality of our situation isn't actually LIKE that if you look closely. I think you'll find that reality is an inclusive flow that includes all of its various designatable phases and states necessarily. So the fact that there're all these separate words doesn't necessarily mean that there're separate, discrete things. There's only one thing; there's only the flow of being. There's only the Tao. You know, whatever you want to call it.

Consciousness puts a splinter there, Consciousness takes it out. Consciousness does everything. Consciousness causes all problems and Consciousness solves all problems.

-My experience gets so clear at times, but then there's this supposed guy who gets into a funk... What would be a good thing to do?

Well, look at what the "funk" is made of. It's made of energy in consciousness, just like a vision of clarity is made of energy in consciousness. Are they really fundamentally different? Why prefer the one to the other? Why do you think clarity IS clarity; why do you think "being in a funk" is NOT clarity?

-Well I know it doesn't feel good...

Right. But instead of defining it as not feeling "good", define it as feeling a certain way; and if you look closely it doesn't even feel a certain way, it feels a continuously changing range of ways, each of which is infinite, subtle, and indescribable. But you collapse all that infinite range of qualities simplistically as "a funk" and "not good".

You're oversimplifying. And you can look at that, if you can, WHILE you're doing it and see if what you're thinking about it is actually TRUE, is an unchallengeable and TOTALLY accurate depiction of what it actually IS.

-I see a series of waves of energies, and then I put a label "depression" on it...

Sure. Even in the midst of depression there are non depressed qualities present. Look at it CLOSELY. And even in the midst of clarity and non-depression there are depressed-like qualities present. Our actual experience is incredibly complex and subtle; it's like a Jackson Pollock canvas or something (laughter). It's actually these splashes of energy with very little coherence; but we're expert at using the blinders of oversimplification to collapse all that down to "Oh, I'm in a pretty good mood right now..."

But that collapsing is a VAST oversimplification of the truth of our experience, which is actually more like a bombardment of complex, instantaneously changing energies being thrown nonstop at our awareness; emotions, sensory noise, a sea of mental energy, and energies that defy classification, but which constantly cascade through our experiencing. There's just a chaos of energies going through my consciousness, and to oversimplify it to just being "we're having a nice conversation" is an absurdity.

But we DO that. So try to notice the reality of what you're ACTUALLY experiencing in realtime. Try to notice that even when you're "depressed", that's a VAST oversimplification of your TRUE state, which defies description. There's a complexity, a chaoticness and an inclusiveness to our different states of mind, that labeling them gives a lie to. We say, "Oh, I'm feeling happy today" or "I'm feeling a bit depressed" or something; but the truth is always infinitely more complex than these oversimplified assessments. And because it's inherently SO much more complex, the simplification is just not true.

So opening to that complexity is also opening to infinity, which is the actual condition of phenomena. Because you're opening to the inherent uncertainty of reality; you can't even KNOW what the states you're experiencing actually are. You CAN'T know; because if you look at them really closely, they open up to more complexity, and more subtlety, without end. It's bottomless. So where do you put your finger down and say, "Yeah, THIS is the state"?

If you look closely into any state it opens into the infinite energy that it actually is. And it's only your conceptual SIMPLIFICATION that you can label as bad or good, you like it or you don't like it. But that labeling is a lie because you're not seeing what it really IS. If you experience the energy intimately as it is, you'll be experiencing infinite chaotic undefinable waves of energy. And what that IS is so out of the league of being able to simply like it or not like it...

We dumb ourselves down. We oversimplify our own experience by not noticing what it really IS, largely through this semantic mechanism of labeling. We're addicted to it. But the antidote is to SEE what it really is. Let ourselves see. We're hypnotized, we don't allow ourselves to really look at it.

-So if I think about doing a feng shui cure in my house to make it better, it already is?

Sure. But look and see for yourself. See the open-ended infinite perfection of the situation, or try the feng shui cure; it doesn't matter either way, it doesn't change what things ARE. If you think in terms of making it "better", "more divine", look and see what THOSE ideas can mean in reality. Just because we have a word in our language doesn't mean it refers to a real "thing".

If you use "divine" the way I do to mean "what is", then clearly everything is divine, because everything that is, is. So you can't possibly make anything MORE divine...

- But feng shui does exist...

Sure. The Klu Klux Klan exists, Naziism exists, people in mental hospitals who think they're Napoleon exist, too. But the fact that they exist as they do doesn't necessarily make their interpretations of reality accurate, doesn't make their stories factual. NO story is factual, THAT'S the fact. Simply because: the elements that make up the story can't be found to exist in reality, in the simple terms in which the story includes them.

You can have a story about your house and your problems and your feng shui and so on, but you can't know for sure what you actually are, what the house actually is, what the problems actually are. It's all speculative; you CAN hypothesize that things might be the way you think they are, you can try your feng shui and see what happens, but you can't KNOW for certain that your story is accurate.

And if you think that your story IS accurate, you've basically fallen into insanity, which is unconditionally believing things are a certain way when you actually don't know for a fact that they are.

-So what would make me call 911 if I was hurt?

Some people don't. But if you're the kind of person that DOES call 911 when you're hurt, then you will. What makes you do ANYTHING? It's the energies which constitute what you actually are at the moment.

-But then she might have the experience of her house being a certain way, and she will put that feng shui ribbon up or whatever, and maybe the energy WILL change in her experience, looking like cause and effect.

Yes, sure. But all that you just said was just ANOTHER story, and each of the elements of the story are of course ALSO undefined and open to interpretation, and you're saying them as if they were certain facts.

-Well, I'm just going on the basis that it seems to have had positive effects for millions of people for many thousand years...

It may have had negative effects for millions of people for thousands of years, too, that just aren't documented. (laughter) If putting red ribbons up in houses was going to be the solution to all our problems, look at the lives of all the people who have done it, and see if they have any problems.

-So with my house, I could evolve to a view that sees there wasn't any problem after all...

Of course. Picture a "realized saint" walking into your house; all they would see is God, not problems.

Fundamentally, singling out supposed "single things" as BEING "single things" is a fallacy, because there are no separate "things" that can be separated out from the continuity of reality. All conditions, objects, actions, exist in a constantly-changing interrelation with everything else; so the field, the continuity of everything, is the only actual "thing".

But that's not a reason to try to not do things, to try feng shui cures etc., that's just an explanation of what doing things actually consists of. You will or you won't put up the red ribbon, and it will or it won't have various results, who can say? But all that will ACTUALLY consist of an unfathomable flow of energy/event that is uninterpretable as it actually is, because it's infinite. And you ARE it.

Our only error is being locked into our interpretation of things, being locked into a particular map, a particular story.

-So even if I do the feng shui cures, put up symbols to improve the flow, that's kind of already what's happening even without them?

Everything whatsoever is a symbol as an expression of the divine, BEING. The shit in the toilet is an expression of the divine, the functioning of reality. The dirt on the floor is an expression of the divine. A situation that's falling apart is an expression of the divine. Because what did it come from? What's it made of? Where does it exist? It's energy in consciousness, co-created with all the universe. ALL phenomena are the expression of the perfection of being,

EVERY aspect of the universe is an expression of that same perfection, including run down houses, wars, all our problems, as well as what we consider beautiful and holy. You can't separate anything out, it's all a whole system, a package deal.

So thinking of things as problems, "bad", OR sacred and holy is just spin-doctoring, making up stories about this whole unfathomable system that reality inalienably IS. The spin-doctoring, positive or negative, CAN'T change the fundamental nature and ongoing functioning of the system of reality, being. It's all already happening, and is NOT amenable to oversimplified explanations.

The "isness" of things as they are is their divine aspect, NOT our take on them. The isness of ourselves is OUR divine aspect. The fact that I exist (as I do) means that I am God; done deal. Just THAT very fact alone, means I've crossed the finish line. I am one with the full system of reality. And of course that applies to "everything else" that exists, too.

So then whatever stories we want to tell about all that is just spinning yarns, right? How can those stories effect the inherent perfection of all being? All they can do is potentially confuse us about it in our ideas.

Because what ELSE is there to talk about in reality than God? You're God, the house is God, you're in the house and having problems, the problems are God, you're going to put up a red ribbon and that's God, it's going to lead to whatever it leads to and THAT'S God; it's all inextricably already ONE BEING functioning as it is, in itself.

So by all means play around with the red ribbon, but SEE, see what it all IS, try and see the context that it is; THAT'S where freedom lies.

-So the problem is not the house or the ribbon or any of that, it's the naming of things as separate entities which enables them to be judged as good or bad...

Yes! THAT'S the real point right there. You can name things all you want, as long as you know it's not the actual condition. It's like naming waves, sitting on the beach watching the waves come in, pointing to them and saying "that wave's George, that wave's Charlie" (Laughter) But of course it's all just the ocean, it's not that this wave is separate from that wave in actuality; it's all just the interaction of the ocean, wind, gravity, temperature, the whole nature of Being in the present moment. You see? So you can name things all you want, just don't believe they're separate entities. THAT'S the fallacy.

-We suffer.

Yes, we suffer, as a result of BELIEVING in our hypothetical interpretation of our experience. We're free to try out all the stories and interpretations we want; as long as we remember they're hypothetical, we won't get trapped by them. Then it just becomes a play, or an exploration of possibilities.

The bottom line is, we can't know where we are, we can't know what we are, we can't know what's happening, other than to experience it as it is. But that opens the door to celebration; that opens the door to letting go; that opens the door to freedom. When we can't know anything, where does that leave us? With a smile on our face and a song in our hearts! (laughter)

-Suppose you think you're in a situation that's bad for you, and you try to do something about it to improve it...

What I'm saying is you have to try to look and see what you're defining the elements of that story to be, what you think the situation seems to be. Then look and see if they really ARE that, if you can KNOW that they're as you're thinking they are. If it turns out you CAN'T know what the elements actually are, the elements that make up the situation, as well as the elements that make up the "you" that you're thinking is IN the situation, that opens the door to seeing it all in new ways that might be useful in solving your supposed problem - from being open to seeing novel approaches to the situation, all the way to seeing that there's NO situation actually, and no "you" that's in it! THAT'S liberation, "enlightenment".

-So that's like the bardo teachings, to see that the appearances aren't a problem...

Yes. It's not that it's NOT a problem, it's that you're thinking of it as a problem because you think the situation is a certain way, and you CAN'T KNOW what it is in reality. Because the reality of every situation is infinitely complex and beyond summing up in some simplistic concept, or even in a very elaborate concept. No matter how subtly we think of anything, we can't possible grasp all the ramifications inherent in what it is. Because everything is infinite, and our thinking is finite.

-There seems to be so many hard-wired urges to satisfy ourselves, and to survive...

Yeah. But that's not YOU, so it's not a problem; it doesn't matter. Whether our minds are driven, or doing our games or whatever, or caught up in some psychological neurosis, is completely irrelevant. The human being, the character that appears as the lead character in my experience, doesn't need to win or lose; it's irrelevant, because it's NOT ME. If it WAS me, then it would matter; but it's not. I'm the perfectly clear, independent, unchanging consciousness that's experiencing all that. And it doesn't matter if this is a comedy or a tragedy, it doesn't affect the experiencer.

The fallacy is identifying with the character. If you're watching a Mel Gibson movie on the screen and you think you ARE Mel Gibson, then you're crazy. You're EXPERIENCING everything that seems to be going on, and you can even have a certain empathy or sympathy with the hypothetical characters that seem to be trapped in the plot, but there's a certainty that YOU'RE NOT ON THAT SCREEN.

Look and see. Look and see if the consciousness that's experiencing your fields of awareness, your life, IS those things, or if those things are IN that consciousness, and it's independent. If you look very closely I think you'll find they're IN the consciousness, and the consciousness is absolutely unhindered by them. When you experience pain, the consciousness is not hurt. It EXPERIENCES the hurt, but IT is not hurt.

-I was thinking about pain.

That's one way you can experience reality.

-Yeah, it seems to be easier somehow to experience that as just energy, while with other sense objects I tend to label them, like that statue I'm seeing there...

You can train yourself to be more aware of your sense of sight as being actually made up of just energy in consciousness by noticing the seeing in a more intimate way, away from specific objects; like for example gazing into the sky. Then if you bring that same subtlety of noticing to the perceiving of a more seductive visual field full of "specific objects", you'll be able to see that the "objects" are actually the same thing, energy in consciousness. It's completely obvious once you see it, because that's what vision, and ALL experiencing, actually IS.

-It's hard to do that with pain as an experience, because I just want it to go away.

That's fine; but the "you" that wants it to go away is not the pure perceiving consciousness that's experiencing both the pain, and the desire to avoid it. Those are both energy-objects, that appear within the pure consciousness. That's the thing to look at; look at what's actually experiencing the pain. Then you'll see there's a perfectly clear, totally honest, completely unbiassed, absolutely infinite consciousness, that's experiencing ALL the energy that shows up in it as your experience, with absolute intimacy.

Whether they're painful or pleasurable, our experiences are being experienced with equal clarity. You experience the pain with exactly as much clarity as you experience sitting here talking now. Our true, actual BEING is that clarity, which is NOT the pain; that clarity is not affected by the pain. The pain appears there, within the clarity, but the clarity does not hurt. But when we identify with our experiences, we forget we're the clarity and we think we're the pain; then WE suffer the pain. It's not like the pain needs to go away, you just need to see clearly that the pain isn't happening to you; it's happening IN you, in the pure awareness that is all you actually always are.

It's just like if you dream that someone's sticking you with a knife, you know? You have the EXPERIENCE of a body being stuck with a knife, but if you know it's a dream, it's not really happening to YOU. It's a dream and you can laugh at it; because it's not YOU. YOU'RE not being threatened, YOU'RE not being damaged or hurt, it's just imagery made of energy appearing in your consciousness.

-So what's EXPERIENCING the pain is what we actually are...

Right. But SEE it, don't just think about it abstractly. See it as it is in realtime and see that you ARE IT, and then all of a sudden you're seeing it from that perspective, and you're LOOKING AT the pain, not BEING the pain.

-I have a fear of not being in control. What's the fear that's coming up? As if I have to hold something together...

Ultimately, if you were EVER in control or ever NOT in control, you did not cause either of those states of affairs. The energies that have made you what you are, which includes your entire history and basically the history of the universe (in terms of all the causes that have ever had an effect on you, and THEIR, causes, and so on), is responsible for those state of affairs. If you're generally a person that has been in control, behaviorally, lets say, that's because that's the kind of person your background has made you. If you're the kind of person that routinely goes OUT of control, THAT'S the kind of person you are. There are plenty of people around who exhibit BOTH arbitrarily defined behavior patterns; but YOU didn't create the control when you WERE in control, and you didn't LOSE control to create the state of being out of control, because both of those are prefigured by what you happen to be at that particular time.

So it becomes a moot point. Whether you're in control, or if you're the kind of person who uncontrollably goes running around naked in public, it's already inherent in what you are, who you are, and you're going to do that anyway; basically, because it's who you are at that time.

Serial killers are going to go out and be serial killers. Why? Because of who they are. They are the kind of person that's motivated to be a serial killer in the circumstances in which they seem to find themselves. People that are "nice" are going to go out and help little old ladies across the street. Why? Because they're the kind of people that are motivated to do that. And people that help little old ladies across the street may be serial killers on the sly. (Laughter)

The point is that all of this mechanism is already in place, it's the natural unfolding of the universe, of reality; so the expressions of it are already prefigured as the show unfolds. So there's no separate you that has to hold control, or a separate you that COULD lose control. You are already the whole mechanism and the whole mechanism is doing what it's doing, which is making you what you are and making you motivated to do what you do. Do you follow that?

-And desire occurs when we don't see the true state of things, and long for completeness, and think we need the object of our desire to achieve that...

The problem isn't the desire, the problem is the sense of incompleteness. You can be functioning from an awareness of completeness and still have desire, but then the desire becomes just an art form. For example, a plant spits out a thousand seeds, and the desire is for every one of them to take root. And each seed tries to. Many of them, perhaps most of them, perhaps none of them, are going to succeed. But the desire is there; and for the plant it's an art form of self-expression. It's the divine energy manifesting as the plant shooting itself out.

-It's like the desire to play music...

Right. But if you have a damaged self image where you think of yourself as separate from the universe, and think you're incomplete and need to do something to fix it, then all of a sudden you're thinking, "Oh my god, I want to do this because it's going to solve my problem... I'm going to be happy, I'm going to get somewhere".

But the problem isn't the desire, or the activity, the problem is the damaged, inaccurate self-image, the model you have of what the universe is and what you are, and what their relationship is.

-We identify ourselves with the incompleteness, but not with the other things in our awareness. How CAN you be incomplete, since you're everything?

Right - but you have to SEE this for yourself, that you're not incomplete. You have to see that there's no such THING as incompleteness. That's the only final antidote for a sense of incompleteness.

-Why do we see that we're the incompleteness, but not that we're also everything else? It's nuts!

Yes. Most people are totally insane; because they believe things that are totally untrue, that they exist as beings that are separate from the universe.

-I see myself compulsively driven by my "little" self, trying to be safe and happy...

Yes, IT will never stop trying to work out its safety, but you're NOT IT. You're what's EXPERIENCING it. The ego doesn't need to stop doing what it does; that's what it's for, that's its job, fighting for safety and so on. But it's not YOU, it's just a spontaneously occurring phenomena in consciousness that you're experiencing. It doesn't need to be different than it is, because there's nothing actually at stake as far as YOU'RE concerned. If your supposed "character" in the drama of "your" life succeeds or fails, what difference does that make to the consciousness experiencing those experiences? It's like worrying about whether the hero in a dream you're having in your sleep lives or dies... What difference does that make to YOU? And even that those supposed conditions (success or failure) are FACTS, is a very oversimplified interpretation of vastly complex and unknowable realities, and hence NOT actually true.

-So I should just laugh at the silly efforts, "There's David trying to find himself"...

Of course. We humans are pathetic creatures, driven unreformably to do what we do. We bumble around as best we can, generally in a mediocre manner at best, then finally we die. That's what human life is. But there's no problem there, because WE AREN'T THAT. WE AREN'T HUMANS. We are the consciousness that EXPERIENCES that, which is not hurt by the pain or healed by the recovery; which is pure and inviolable, infinite and open-ended, ever-present consciousness/intelligence, WITHIN WHICH the drama of the universe takes place.

-I'm confused about consciousness abiding in clarity, and then seems to NOT be abiding in clarity...

That confusion itself is actually experienced by perfectly clear consciousness with perfect, absolute clarity. When you're confused, you know it with absolute clarity. WHAT knows it? HOW do you know you're confused? THAT'S you; THAT knowing clarity is you, and it never changes, it never fades. Murkiness and confusion happen IN experience, but the consciousness that EXPERIENCES those conditions is always absolutely clear and perfect, like a dust-free mirror, that all this is reflected in.

When you're confused, you know it for a fact. When you're in joy, you know it for a fact. When you're sick, you know it for a fact. When you're asleep, you know that for a fact, whether or not you know you know it. But you DO. The knower that's experiencing it is experiencing it. If you DIDN'T experience it, you wouldn't feel "I slept last night", you'd feel "I didn't exist last night". Everything happens IN experience; you are the experiencER.

-But what about our personalities?

That's a very good question. Our personalities don't need to go away, don't need to be fixed, don't need to be repressed; don't need to be perfected in order to see reality. We just have to see beyond them and see what they actually ARE, what they're made of. All our quirks, our neuroses, the imperfections of our natures that were beaten into us and drilled into us as we grew up, don't need to be fixed. They aren't the problem. They may be a distraction, but they aren't the problem.

And when you see reality, you see WHAT those things are, how they exist in their own context. They are the history of our manifestations, like scars. They exist as echoes of events having been experienced, but they don't block or impede your being, even if they contribute shape to your experience. If I lost a hand or something, that would inhibit some of my activities, but it wouldn't stop me from BEING me. Likewise, our psychological quirks aren't an impediment to seeing what we already are, and have always been, or to BEING that.

-It's strange how there seem to be these dualities, matter and consciousness, and science and spirituality...

Well, spirituality is a big lie. The word is based on a lie; what is "spirit"? Spirit is supposed to be that which is other than matter or is superior to matter, the solution to matter, or that from which matter came, and so on. But nothing comes from anything, everything simply IS what it is. Consciousness, experience, matter, ALL things are the functioning of the one reality. So there's no spirituality other than THIS (waves to indicate the present situation); this is spirituality.

The idea that spirituality is some state that you get to through effort and behaving in a certain way, doing elaborate spiritual practices, stop all wars, only eat vegetables, and so on, is a common notion. All those behaviors are legitimate ways of living our lives as expressions of our natures, but will you BE anything different after you do them than you are before that? What are you now? What you are now fundamentally, on the most basic level, is what you will be then, and have ALWAYS been.

THAT'S what spirituality is; spirituality is the true reality of what being is, what everything is, what the universe is, what YOU are.

Reality is always itself. Reality is always real. And THAT'S what spirituality is. It's reality; it's already accomplished, we don't have to do anything to make it more perfect or complete. It IS perfect and complete in its very nature; and we are one with it, also perfect and complete. If you don't know that intimately, you can investigate further to see if it's indeed so.

-It's like a bunch of fish thinking they have to search for water...

It's exactly like that. We feel we need to search only because we don't know that we already have it, already ARE it. It's amazing.

But this mechanism of devaluing being itself, which comes as a reaction to OVER valuing certain aspects of experience, successes and achievements, is the culprit. We devalue what we ARE. We devalue consciousness. It's obvious, if you look closely, that you ARE consciousness. You are what is experiencing your experience, which is what we're calling consciousness. And we simply don't notice how amazing, infinite, complete, full, and whole that consciousness that we are is; we fixate on its expressions as experience and get all caught up in that soap opera, and get distracted from the fundamental FACT; all being is nothing other than this amazing consciousness, the essence of fullness and perfection, and WE ARE THAT. But we usually devalue it. We think of consciousness as some accidental biochemical byproduct of our bodies, our brains, and that it comes and goes, like a flickering flame. And that it's only useful to enable us to go achieve our goals in the worlds we think we're experiencing. But that's sloppy thinking.

-When we think of consciousness as our spiritual goal, we think it's a specific thing we have to focus on...

We fixate on one thing and think, "Oh, THAT'S consciousness, let me focus on it and go after it"; but we're ignoring the fact that everything ELSE is consciousness, too. And if we can notice what we already have, what we already ARE, maybe we'd notice that we don't have to go after anything, we already HAVE it inalienably. It spontaneously appears continuously, unstoppably, intimately; we don't need to go get it.

We think of some wonderful one-pointed yoga practice, thinking that if we go to the Himalayas and do this for twenty years we'll achieve something wonderful. But WHATEVER that is will still be just energy appearing in consciousness, which is all that was ever happening even before spending your life doing the practice. By all means do what interests you if you can in life, but it will be just self-expression; you can never modify what you ARE; the pure being/functioning of reality itself, of the universe itself.

-So where's choice? Or is that just a waste of time?

It's not a waste of time. Choice is just a way of describing functioning, but any way of describing functioning doesn't capture the way it really is. It can't, right? Because any description is partial. We experience functioning, we experience motivation, we experience impulse that we act on or don't act on, and all that is what we refer to as choices.

But if we look closely are they REALLY choices? Do we have CONTROL over all the energies and impulses and urges that come up in us? Do we have control of SOME of them? Well, who knows? But whatever it is, it all boils down to us functioning as the entities that we are; and the entities we are ARE the entities we are because ultimately of the nature of the universe. So again, it all collapses down to WHAT IS.

Everything is an expression of the one system, including us and our functioning and all our complexities. All the aspects of our social functioning, our social interaction, and all of that. It's ALL an expression of the same thing. It's the only show in town. Our politics is an expression of the same thing, our wars, our financial concerns, our concerns with our social status; all these things are just expressions of... It's humans being humans, and humans ARE humans because the universe MADE them that way. Describe it as "it evolved that way", or "the energies come together that way", or however you want to model it.

Again, we can't KNOW what it actually is definitively, it's beyond modeling; modeling reduces it to something simplistic. But you can't get away from the fundamental FACT; and anything and everything whatsoever is an expression of that fact. In terms of OUR functioning, or the functioning of inanimate objects; anything. Every quark in the universe is dancing around doing exactly what the nature and functioning of the universe is making it do. Right? Including those that happen to be part of an animate system like us, or those that are part of supposedly inanimate things like this carpet.

The forces that put these atoms here (points to hand) are the same forces that put these atoms here (points to table). So it's ALL an expression of the same system. You can't ultimately separate any of it out. Where does that leave free will, choice? As one simplistic description of that functioning.

-So war is not bad...

Of course not. If you don't like it, and you want to try to do something about it, go for it. Because that's not bad either.

-And that's freedom.

Yes, exactly, that's freedom. And what it IS, is the freedom of things to be what they already are. It's the freedom that's inherent in what is.

-So we're back to energy in consciousness.

Yeah! Isn't it satisfying to feel consciousness experiencing being, directly? Experience is experiencing itself as reality. (claps hands) They are one. There's no intermediary, no separation or distance. What we experience is what's real; we're experiencing reality. You know? It's ULTIMATELY satisfying; it's Shiva in union with Shakti. It's the divine marriage.

-Can you talk about the certainty?

Not really... It consists of the OBVIOUSNESS of the nature of being, directly perceived. It's not a theory or a faith or a hope or a conviction, just the obvious, immediate fact of WHAT IS. Being is a fact, and I AM that fact. It's what I am, entirely, and that is immediately obvious to me. It's what all things, this entire universe, is.

-Was there a time where you had no certainty, then from that time on you did?

Yes. But please understand that there's not any substantial difference between one's state pre-certainty, and post-certainty. You don't gain anything new, or transform from one thing into another thing. It consists of just seeing things in their true perspective (which turns out to be perspective less); that they've actually ALWAYS been in all along.

It's like one of those optical illusion puzzles where you look at it and you look at it, and you just can't see what you're supposed to be able to see, and then all of a sudden bang! You get it! Then you're not actually SEEING anything different than you were looking at all along, but all of a sudden the perspective is there, and you can see what the puzzle is all about. And once you see it, it becomes easy to see it again whenever you want to look at it.

So it's not an actual change, there's no new information; it's a matter of the true perspective, the true order of things. We don't know the actual structure or order of things until we find certainty, then it becomes immediately obvious. Once we find certainty we KNOW, inalienably; it's not a matter of argument, opinion, or discussion, just the simple fact of SEEING what the true "proportion of things" is, which paradoxically could be said to be NO order.

That's what I mean by certainty; knowing what's valuable. What's valuable is BEING; what's valuable is what we already are, what everything already is; the "isness" of the present moment, right here, right now. It's the pot of gold at the end of the rainbow. And it's so obvious; everything is in it, everything IS it, everything comes from it and goes to it, everything functions and behaves as it does BECAUSE of it. What could be more valuable? It's not elaborate itself, but it appears as the unending elaboration of the universe, of our experience.

-Was there a moment, or moments, when you especially realized the nature of reality?

Sure. I've been seeing it all my life, but I didn't REALIZE I was seeing it; that's the case with all of us. What blinds us to its true nature is our frames of reference, of beliefs, which trap us into experiencing our experience from within them conceptually. But reality is actually WITHOUT a frame of reference; and to see it as it IS, you have to drop ALL frames of reference.

When I was with my teacher, on one particular occasion I SAW what he actually was, and I saw that he KNEW what he was. And when I saw that, I saw what I was, and I saw that HE knew what I was. It was relationship and communion beyond anything I had ever experienced previously, a self-validating open view of being in reality. I can't possibly describe it beyond that. It was a completely clear, shared understanding of the nature of reality; of what I am. I am reality, my entire being is reality.

It was a very specific event, that instantly gave me perspective on all my previous experience, gave me a reference-less perspective that is the TRUE perspective. I had ALWAYS known that, but I didn't KNOW that I knew it because I was confused by all these supposed referential world views that had been thrown at me all my life or that I had formulated.

-It took you twenty-four years from the time you "saw" until you finally settled into it...

Well, you see it when you see it. And then you're able to stay with seeing it, when you have successfully processed your way through the confusion that KEEPS you from seeing "IT". And that's a matter of your personal karma, the patterning of your unfoldment, how long that process takes.

So when YOU get clearer on the things that are stopping you from seeing, is when you see it more and more. You have to notice what's tripping you up. And perhaps the best way to get clarity on what's tripping you up, is to keep tripping on it.

WE are our own impediments. The structures of our beliefs, regarding what we think we are and what the world is, are our impediments; because they're unconscious and we don't know they're there, but we believe they're REAL. They trip us up by making us goal oriented. The problem is ALWAYS goal orientation; and there is in actuality no goal, what IS in this present moment is the goal, and we already "have it"; there is nothing else.

We're either pushing towards a goal, or avoiding one; Buddha nailed that one. Second noble truth, bang! "The cause of suffering is attraction and aversion." Wanting some "things" and not wanting other "things".

Basically what it means is you're imaginarily separating supposed entities out of non-entifiable, continuous reality. Which points to another cardinal tenet of Buddhism, annata, "no-self". No entities. No "things". There are no entities, there are no selves.

It's actually insanity, believing in things that are not there, to believe in separate entities within this non-quantifiable, continuous reality that we actually live within and ARE. But we're ignorant of that state of affairs; we think the facts support our beliefs in separate things. It's the common point of view; "Of course there are separate things - there's you, there's me, there's this room, etc. What are you talking about, are you nuts?" But it's actually the other way around! THAT'S the "nutty" perspective. To have enough clarity to see that, comes when it comes. But the things that KEEP us from seeing that are our subtle beliefs and our subtle attachments concerning what we are, what the world is, and what to do about whatever we think those are.

The primary fallacy is to think that we exist as separate beings. THEN comes defining ourselves. So we have an unconscious picture of ourselves as "this", as something, that is always relative to a world we think we live in, as we think THAT is. Then comes the problem of what to DO about that, ourselves as we think we are in the world as we think it is.

Then we get critical, wanting ourselves or the world to be different than we think they are, and we start to worry, struggle, punish ourselves, and blame the world. All for a case of mistaken identity! (laughter) "This poor me ought to be rich. This unenlightened me ought to be enlightened." Then we're unconsciously flagellating ourselves for not being what we think we aren't.

But it's ALL a fallacy. We aren't the FIRST thing, "unenlightened", that we think we ARE, and we already are the SECOND thing, "enlightened", that we think we're NOT. Because we're really actually and inherently everything, it's all already a done deal.

If you create the idea of separate entities, you're creating lies, falsehoods; and ultimately they'll trip you up.

-What makes one person become a pessimistic existentialist, and another person say, "It's all god and ever-blessed"?

What makes anything be anything? It's the flow of events. It's the expression of the causal matrix of all of being, flowering as any "particular event". Anything is what it is because of the way EVERYTHING is; and everything "else" has impacted it to be that way. Right? How could it be otherwise? Everything is embedded in the whole, in all circumstance, and reacts to those circumstances as it all changes, as it constantly does. It's just a summing of vectors; what happens is the combination of all the influences that produce it.

I could be described as being the way I am because of the genetic structure I got from my parents, and the impact of all the accidental circumstances that happened to me during my life experience. The combination of ALL those things brought me here, now, doing what I'm doing. And the same for everybody, anybody.

-Is there any meaning to talk about effort or focus?

What do you think?

-(Laughs) I get stuck in efforting a lot...

Look at it this way. If there IS effort or focus, it has to be a natural expression of you being yourself, which again is a natural outgrowth of the functional entity that you are, the universe, reacting to circumstances as the universe presents itself. Right?

-Yeah...

So it's all basically a done deal, in the sense that it can't really be different, unless the circumstances evolve or your functional nature evolves, both of which are happening nonstop. So in other words if you're exerting effort or struggling with things, that's because the universe has made you to be an entity at this point in time who is motivated to do those sorts of things.

So even your effort isn't effort, because it's caused by the universe. The universe is doing it; the universe is the causal agent and the substance which is doing it, it's just showing up as "you", and you're interpreting it as YOUR effort, or YOUR struggle. But the effort and the struggle are prefigured in what you ARE and what your circumstances are, and what THEY are is prefigured in what the whole universe is! Can you see that?

-Yeah...

So the onus is not on you to struggle or not struggle, to have focus or NOT to have focus; all that will inevitably take care of itself. And how could you stop it? If you COULD stop it that would also be an expression of the universe doing it. In other words, the universe is doing everything. Everything that's being done is being done by IT. We're not doing anything; we're off the hook, we're out of the loop.

-It's being done through us?

Of course. And there's no "us" that it's being done "through", there's no "us", it's just being done, period. We interpret it as being done through us because we think "we're" the owners of our experience; but actually there is no "we" who own it, experience just IS. We define ourselves as existing because of the obvious fact of experience happening. We assume there must be a "me" that is doing the experiencing; in actuality experience experiences itself.

-So if we let it flow through us, if there's no resistance...

Yeah, no resistance. If there's no resistance then we can begin seeing reality happening as it is, because we're not invested in the outcome of doership. It's like if you're at a horserace and you have a lot of money bet on one horse, then you're distracted by that investment, obsessed with following that one horse, excited when it seems to be ahead, and worried when it seems to lag behind. But if you don't have any money on it, don't have a preference, you can just sit back and watch the event unfold impartially, admire ALL the horses without worry; you get to see the big picture.

And it's the same in our lives. If we're fixated on specific things, it causes us to have tunnel vision. But if we're in nonresistance, basically letting events flow as they ARE, then our perspective broadens naturally and we can see the whole pattern of events, the nonlinear interactions that shape and indeed constitute all "things".

-Is that why Neem Karoli Baba didn't get high when he took all that LSD from Ram Das?

How do you know he didn't get high? (laughter) Let me answer that by saying this. Experience is always being what it ACTUALLY is; and a person who knows what their experience actually is, is always experiencing the same thing; energy in consciousness. And is always experiencing its patterns as constantly changing and without reference point.

So the difference between being sober and being blasted on LSD is essentially nonexistent, for a person who's experiencing the reality of their sensation. Because you're ALWAYS experiencing flashing lights and changing colors and shapes moving and all this; always! But we ignore it, we dumb ourselves down and fixate on our story. "Oh, I'm in a room, talking with other people, no more than that, and that's all that's happening."

-Is that what you mean by reference?

Yes. Exactly. The reference point is definitions. If I'm not defining what's going on, then what IS going on? This field of crazy lights and sounds and energies in consciousness. You know, and when you take LSD you get a field of crazy lights and sounds and energies in consciousness. How is THAT any different? (laughter)

-Years ago I got on "Magic Mountain" at Disneyland, because I heard the monks would meditate on that ride. I sat in the front and had no expectations about what I would experience, so it was as if nothing happened. If there's no expectation, frame of reference, or resistance, there's no ride.

Exactly. Resistance creates the world, creates concrete reality. Nonresistance reveals true reality. Nonresistance allows us to see God. Because then you don't have a reference point, you're wide open to what IS. That's the Dzogchen view; no resistance, no reference point. It's just open being. WHAT IS it? What is it? You don't even ASK the question let alone answer it, as the answer is obvious and unsayable.

-So how do we get here?

How indeed. Good question. HOW we are, WHAT we are, WHY we are, WHERE we are, WHEN we are, and WHO we are all have the same answer, they are all the same question. And the answer is the Mystery, the Divine, God, Consciousness, the Universe, Reality itself; which we ARE and everything IS, and has always been and will always be. End of story. Any name we give it is moot because it's beyond defining or modeling.

But IT is the substance of everything, IT is the motive of everything, it's the cause of everything, it's the result of everything. Any quality whatsoever you want to query about it, IT IS THAT. It's the one thing. It's its own agent and its own substance. The universe creates itself, the universe experiences itself, the universe is the substance of itself, and the universe dissolves back into itself. It's like a snake eating its tail.

So the answer to any question you can ask about it is the same; IT. Everything comes from this one functioning, and consist of this one functioning, so all explanations boil down to this one functioning itself.

-It's hard to talk about this, but sometimes the words come together in just the right way...

Well, my approach is if you throw enough words out, kind of like a million monkeys pounding on a million typewriters, sooner or later you'll say something meaningful... (laughter)

The problem is there's NO way to definitively say this stuff. It's impossible. It's unsayable. So trying to talk about it is an absurdity at worst, and an art form at best. But knowing that, and making the attempt anyway, if we dance around it enough, some of our talk may knock up against something real.

But even though we can't talk about reality definitively, we CAN look at it.

And so we're talking around it, but hopefully this talking around it encourages us to look at it. Because we CAN see it directly. In fact, we've never seen anything ELSE. Anything we've ever experienced whatsoever IS the energy of reality. Immediately. And so we're always seeing it, we're never seeing anything but.

But you can't describe it, you can't talk about it, you can't define it. The definitions and the descriptions will ALWAYS fall short, because IT is infinite; hence indescribable in finite terms, and our language implies finite elements. If I asked you to describe conclusively what your experience is, how could you? Look at what your experience is. There're fields of sensory experience, there're fields of mental experience, there're fields of emotional experience, and fields of experience that can't be said to fall into any of those categories. And calling them "fields" is arbitrary; what does THAT mean? We can call it energy in consciousness... but is that a description, or just a pathetic attempt at one that begs the question? WHAT exactly do we mean by "energy"? What do we mean by "consciousness"?

-And then all the words are subject to interpretation of what they mean to me, or to you...

Of course. It's all telling stories, it's all telling lies.

There seems to be a promise in spirituality that once you "get it" you'll no longer have to experience these other states, because you'll always be in bliss...

The way the truth of "spirituality" solves the problems of our life, is to show us that the way our life has ALWAYS been, is in actuality NOT a problem. The problem is us defining certain states or conditions as "problems". And we define problems because of attachment and aversion. True spiritual realization is seeing for a fact that the way things are is not a problem - once you see nakedly the way they, and YOU, ACTUALLY are. You see that there's no one for it to be a problem FOR in actuality.

So when you see that there's no problem, of course that solves your problems. But it doesn't solve them by SOLVING them; it solves them by showing you that there never were any in the first place.

-For nine months I had an experience of bliss and clarity; it felt like being home...

Well you WERE home. And look and see if you aren't home now too, and always have been. You were noticing it then, and sometimes you may not be noticing it; but when you DON'T see it, it's not because it's not true. And you can KNOW it even when you're not "seeing" it, which is what true "spiritual" realization is. Realization is knowing the true state of affairs, and that it is always what it is; and always has been, and always will be, whatever we're seeing or NOT seeing.

It will always look different than it has. It'll look like you being sick and in pain when you're on your death bed: being blissed out when you're in a meditational high: like you being in a funk when you have a bad interaction with someone, or whatever. But that's what reality looks like. But it's ALWAYS pure energy in consciousness. And when you realize this conclusively, there's nothing more to realize. But when we start separating out states and defining them, saying "this state is this state" and "that state is that state", it's a fallacy. It is true in a way that the states of experience that you have will evolve. It's true that caterpillars turn into butterflies; it's NOT true that caterpillars are better than butterflies. So you will have evolution of states of mind, and those states may assume patterns at times that you might define as a certain ascendancy or something. But it's NOT true that any state of mind is better than any other state of mind. They're all aspects of the same thing; your being. Whatever the pattern of your unfoldment looks like, that's the pattern of your unfoldment. But when you get completely "unfolded", you're not ACTUALLY any more unfolded than you ever were. It's just that then you're manifesting that aspect of your being, which you always are. When you're in the middle of it, you're manifesting THAT phase of your being. It's always an aspect of your being, which you always ARE the completeness of. And THAT'S what spiritual realization is; it's seeing the truth that you always are, and have always been, the inherent fulness of your being, regardless of what aspect of it you happen to be unfolding at the moment. And then you're always home. It's just that home looks different at different times, and you don't get attached to any particular version.

-You can't have a judgment about anyone else's state of spiritual unfoldment...

Of course not, how could you? You CAN'T know. You can't even have a clear understanding of whatever "level" YOU'RE at, let alone have a clear understanding of where anyone else is at. But that's very superficial; because in actuality there are no "levels", only mystery.

-There does seem to be a myth that with spiritual realization, there are no more difficult experiences, it'll be all butterflies and rainbows...

Well, sometimes it's butterflies and rainbows, and sometimes it isn't. But it's NEVER anything other than the divine. And seeing THAT fact is realization. Being attached to pretty states is an immature understanding.

-There's also the myth that everyone will become a spiritual teacher when they get to a certain level...

People do what their nature dictates. And even people who become spiritual teachers may not be gifted at it. It's like anything else. Everyone manifests the talents and deficiencies that they inherently embody, and that persists as long as they're manifesting as anything, whether they're "spiritually realized" or not.

There's a lot of history of criticizing spiritual teachers for being a certain way or for NOT being a certain way; behaviors, sex, money, etc., and all that's an absurdity; because the genuineness of their realization and the effectiveness of their functioning as spiritual teachers is independent of their behavior in human terms. They may be incompetent in other areas, but still have a genuine realization. And vice-versa, you may have a really effective teacher that doesn't have a genuine realization, but they gather many followers. Look at the Jim Jones effect, and so on.

It's like all of human functioning, everyone just does the best they can, we just work with what we've got at the time and have a go at it. And that's ALWAYS the path. We get up tomorrow and do the best we can.

-It seems like until we realize our true nature, we're stuck in fight or flight, because all our ideas of our situation are based in defending or manipulating the ego...

That's ego. Ego is our soap opera, ego is our story; the story we tell ourselves about who we are and what we're doing. The ego story includes all kinds of suppositions. It includes suppositions about what you are, what the world is like, projections of what could happen in various situations, and so on. You could check down the list of THOUSANDS of suppositions that are inherent in that whole story.

And that's part of our human functioning; creating these stories. But when we reach a certain point in our unfoldment, we start to question them, and begin to look at all that. And eventually we may not need all those stories. Which DOESN'T necessarily mean we'll stop telling them altogether; we just will stop believing in them.

-So the freedom is to KNOW that they're stories...

Yes. But it's all a part of our functioning. It's what humans do, it's part of us being what we are. And it's not a problem that we do that, it's just our nature. Like as caterpillars we crawl around and eat leaves; then one day we get the urge and we crawl up on a leaf and spin a cocoon and then we fly out, transformed creatures, and we mate and die. Every aspect of our functioning at all levels of our development is a natural part of that whole development, culminating (perhaps) in realization of our true nature. And is that the end?...

-But then (after enlightenment), can we still explore our life, still have our preferences, or what?

Life becomes like walking through a museum; seeing myriads of different kinds of beauty, in different aspects of things, which are all miraculously beautiful and amazing and profoundly meaningful. Some may resonate with you more than others, but you don't need anything from them, or to avoid them either. They're there, they have their beauty as expressions of Pure Being. You get to enjoy that beauty and move on, and there's more beauty, nothing but beauty. It's a continual cascade of different textures of amazement.

BUT, you have to see that fundamental miracle first for yourself.

You have to see the miraculous nature of your being. It's not hard to see; the only thing keeping us from seeing it is our own cussedness in getting caught up and invested in all of our bullshit, believing our own lies.

Seeing it can be like a trick. You know those computer-generated pictures that look like fuzzy abstract patterns, but then once you "get" the way to look at them, you can see the 3d image hidden inside? It's actually plain to see, but you won't be ABLE to see it until you stumble on the WAY to see it; then it's easy. That's a perfect analogy for seeing reality as it actually is; because after all, you're looking at it right now, but maybe you just don't see it. Right? Then suddenly you stumble on the right way to view it, then all of a sudden, BANG! There it is!

And it's not that it wasn't there before, you just weren't SEEING it, you weren't looking at it right. But it's a trick. And it's a trick that you can learn, it's a trick of perspective you can have pointed out to you, and you can explore it and wrestle with it, and then one day suddenly you GET it, and you SEE. It's definitely a trick, and the more you explore it and the more you familiarize yourself with it, you can do it easier, deeper, faster, etc. Once you SEE it, everything becomes infinitely interesting and you no longer have a need for things to come out one way or another, so it's like watching an amusing show. You're interested in where the plot's going to go, but you don't really need it to go this way rather than that way.

-Have you read Jed McKenna?

Oh yes! I love his books, he's a hoot.

-And I guess he doesn't actually exist...

Well the guy that wrote those books, whoever he is, knows what he's talking about.

-What do you think about his process of spiritual autolysis?

It's right on the money. It's one way of describing the process of entering into "spiritual" realization.

-It's kind of like what we're doing here, we're just not writing it down...

Of course. And the fact that you're even motivated to come to meetings like this means that you're in that process, you're examining things.

-But isn't it ego that brought us all here?

No, ego doesn't bring us anywhere. Ego is a symptom.

-Ego isn't what is propelling and motivating our behavior?

No, of course not. Motivation arises from what we ARE. And ego is just a superstructure that we spin around those urges that come up spontaneously from our being. It may subvert some of the energy, but it doesn't have any motivations of its own. It claims them and tries to own them; it says "I decided this" and I'M doing that". But that's a lie, because the actual doing, the actual urge, comes out of the essence of our being, which is one with the being of the universe.

-So we're being breathed, we're being moved, we're being thought, everything...

Of course.

-So the ego's just the story...

Yes. But it's not a CONSCIOUS story, that's the problem. So we believe in it because we have all sorts of little unconscious assumptions which we assume are true. We may assume the material world actually exists; we may assume our body actually exists, and that we are IN it; we make all these assumptions, which have implications which we react to as if they were true, which puts a lot of stress and strain on our emotional nature; then we feel that we're working hard and suffering.

It's like someone that's really been sucked into a soap opera; "Oh no! Eleanor's been raped and Dr. Ben is going to get away with it, and story, story, story... It's terrible!" And that's what we do ourselves. The actual fact is we can't KNOW what our situation is; so all these stories are just hypotheses, and we torture ourselves needlessly by believing in them as if they were TRUE unquestioningly.

So it's all "what if". IF the world existed and IF I existed and IF I was a male human being and IF I had the history I think I had, THEN, I would be a failure at this and a partial success at that, and I would be getting old, and I would be going to die soon, and I would be wondering what the point of my life was... BUT, all that is dependent upon these "if's". And if I look at those "if's", and if I can't know whether they're true as I think them to be, then the entire story collapses.

-So it goes back to Ramana, and who is it that is thinking that?

Yeah! Who's thinking it, what's it made of, where is it happening... The point is to ask any question that makes you investigate WHAT'S ACTUALLY GOING ON in this being of the present moment, to try to see it as it ACTUALLY is, and not just through the haze of our suppositions. What IS it? What's going on here, right now? Who's experiencing it? What's it made of? Look at any of those questions, and you'll be looking at reality. And once you see it directly, reality will teach you what it is. Directly, not verbally or conceptually. It can do this because it is inherently made of pure intelligence. When you start looking at what God is, God will start teaching you what it is. But until then, we're caught up in our pie-in-the-sky fantasies, and we can't learn anything about reality.

-So sometimes I'm looking at it, and I see that it's energy in consciousness, and then other times I look at it and don't know WHAT it is... Is that a better way to look into it?

Yes. Drop all reference points and just be nakedly with it, without any preconceptions or labeling.

-I see it and think about all the ways I've been told it is, but then sometimes I'm with it and I don't KNOW what it is.

THAT'S the place to be. That's good. Just stay with it, and open to that not-knowing; and it will teach you, it'll reveal itself to you as it is. Gradually, almost by osmosis. Be with it as openly and as unconditionally as you can, and it will reveal itself. But the less you think you know about it, the fewer expectations you bring to it, the more you'll be able to see it as it is. It will teach you, it will show you.

All this crap I spew out here in Satsang, I don't sit at home thinking about what to say. (laughter) What happens is IT teaches me what it is; I look at it, and it expresses itself through the words I use. It's self-revealing; it teaches what it is. But you'll see what it is more accurately, the fewer preconceptions you bring to it; otherwise you'll just be seeing your preconceptions, and just be in another state of illusion.

-I was at Ammachi's ashram, and they were telling me all this stuff, and I felt like, "screw this! This doesn't ring true for me..."

The process of coming to the point of saying "screw this", means that you're learning a bit about your truth; which is what it's all about. It's about learning YOUR truth, the truth of what you are. YOU'RE who has to see reality; YOU have to know it as you actually do, NOT as someone tells you it is. Whether you learn your truth positively, like "THIS is it!", or negatively, like "This is NOT it for me", it's a big revelation to know what it is for YOU. All our lives is our spiritual path; but when you really dig down to the the primal aspect of what it is FOR YOU, that's the big thing.

-I love how you say we've got the power of the universe backing us up...

Yeah. Every occurrence whatsoever, it IS the power of the universe that's doing it, backing it up. Everything. We're off the hook. We're totally not responsible. The universe is doing it.

This very investigation we're doing here, all this questioning, the universe is doing it. And IT'S what is EXPERIENCING the doing of it. And when we're ignorant and caught up in our stories, the universe is doing THAT too. You know?

There's nothing BUT enlightenment. When you shit in the toilet, that's enlightenment. The act is, the substance is, the entire thing is. There's nothing but enlightened being. When you put an "s" at the end of that, "Enlightened

Beings", that's a fallacy because we're creating entities where there are none. There are no entities. The reality of Being is just itself. Being. It's an unfathomable infinite entity. No "me", no "you". It's infinitely variegated. Always different than itself. Always becoming different than it was. It looks as if there are a whole lot of things that we seem to be surrounded by, but all of that stuff is actually the unfoldment of one thing, just like all the "objects" in a dream. When you dream, it's an unfoldment of one thing. The dream is a perfect analogy. But if you're dreaming and you don't KNOW you're dreaming, you think you're in an actual situation. Maybe monsters chasing you and you have to run away because you're afraid they're going to kill you. If you KNOW you're dreaming, you know you can't die, and that there is no monster, there are no "things". You're experiencing the monster, but you know it's not really there, YOU aren't actually IN that apparent situation. And it isn't actually even a "situation"...

It's exactly the same with all this. We define all these so called entities into existence including ourselves. We DEFINE ourselves into existence. The EXPERIENCE is obviously there, but we define the experience as being centered around these supposedly real bodies, which supposedly exist in an objectively existing space and so on. If you look really closely, there's no evidence for that. Using Occamm's razor, throw it out. It's unnecessarily complicated. If you look at life as being a dream, it actually makes a lot more sense and the evidence supports it. Of course, you can get all sorts of really elaborate theories. You can get as complicated as you want without HARD evidence, which is what we're already doing for the most part.

The point is to take a skeptical look at what the evidence ACTUALLY supports, and ultimately the evidence supports nothing more than the fact that BEING IS. And being is identical with experience. Experience is. You can't say that experience is happening to SOMEONE. You can't say the experience consist OF something in particular. But it's OBVIOUSLY happening, whatever it is. And we define ourselves into existence out of that fundamental fact, and a world into existence out of that fundamental fact. Political beliefs, success and failure, death and life, and on and on... We make all these incredibly complex stories that we tell ourselves about what is happening, but ALL of it is just resting on the fact that experience is existing; and if you look closely, we cannot actually know what the heck that really is. You CAN'T know what experience is. That's a fact. You CAN'T. It's unknowable. It's unfathomable. You can't meaningfully, consistently supply any clear definition of it. Because you're building on a cloud, on a dream. You're just making leaps of faith, assumptions, which you're free to do. Make all the assumptions you want. But you may be building yourself into an imaginary box.

-I wonder about the statement from Descartes "I think therefore I am", and Niche's "God is dead"; that's misinterpreted...

Basically ANY philosophy is inherently wrong, because the map will always be less than the terrain. A philosophy is a picture of reality, therefore wrong; since reality is inherently unpicturable except by itself. Which is why all spiritual traditions are doomed to failure; because you can't paint an accurate picture of reality. No matter how detailed you get, how clear you are, you're still going to be inaccurate. Reality is not susceptible to being captured in finite terms, because it's infinite.

If you're really serious about spirituality, about reality, it's important to understand the way that maps are useless. If you really want to find reality, you have to throw the maps out the window, which means: all conceptual thinking, the notion that a symbol refers to something, the notion that this symbol equals that object, the door is that and the floor is this. You've got to throw them all out the window and without any reference point whatsoever, look around and see where you are. And THEN you can begin to see things as they are. But if you have any kind of conceptual map, you're seeing the map and not the terrain. You'll be selectively pulling out evidence that supports your map, and subliminally ignoring the evidence that doesn't, no matter how open minded you try to be.

-That's a brilliant idea. So as long as you're looking at the map...

That's ALL you're looking at. Which is what most people do with spirituality. Most people don't learn about reality, they learn a spiritual lifestyle. Buddhists generally don't learn to truly SEE Buddha or reality, they learn about being a Buddhist. They learn the language, chants, practices, ways of appearing to act. They're learning "shtick"; they're not learning about what Buddhism was about. Buddha was trying to say "Hey gang, this is Reality, look at it."

-It's not about counting your beads...

Basically, 99 percent of "spirituality" is leaning maps, learning lifestyles, adopting a new lifestyle. For most people it's not about trying to find actual reality AS IT IS, which is what enlightenment IS actually. But it's about self-image and status, feeling good about oneself by being able to think of oneself as "spiritual", or at least TRYING to be "spiritual"; or perhaps feeling one is better than other people who AREN'T as "spiritual" as one thinks oneself. What does any of that have to do with noticing reality?

I define enlightenment as seeing reality nakedly, as it is, without a map. Or with maps, but not being stuck in them. It's not like we need to discard the maps, you can carry around as many maps as you want, as long as you KNOW they're not the real thing. You don't need to give up English just because all words in English are lies. All words are INHERENTLY lies, to the extent that they deviate from reality because they cannot capture reality accurately as it is.

The trick is to not confuse the two, the map and the terrain. There's an EPIDEMIC of confusing the two, people looking at maps and thinking they're looking at reality. And they argue about their maps and they fight about their maps and they kill each other.

-It's like we're tourists in Ireland and we're all looking at the map at how beautiful it is instead of putting the map down and seeing Ireland for real.

Sure, You see that with tourists. They have to get out their guide book to see what it is they're looking at. Put the book down and just LOOK at it. Don't 'know' what it is, just SEE what it is. The book will give you all kinds of good information, but it will not BE the thing. It'll be missing infinite amounts of information. You can carry around the Encyclopedia Britannica about this particular object, and it will still be missing infinite amounts of information about it, because the map inherently falls far short of the terrain.

Look at language. We use words, and we're in the subliminal habit of thinking our language is more or less accurate. If we try to tell the truth, we can try use these words accurately to the best of our ability, really try and call a spade a spade; but the actual fact is, it's IMPOSSIBLE because LANGUAGE DOES NOT CORRESPOND TO REALITY, except in the most accidental of ways. I can say, that's a door, this is a rug, this is me. What am I saying about what they really ARE?

In using these names I'm compartmentalizing it, this infinite unique thing that only exists at this infinite time and location and space, and it's already gone and transformed into something else as soon as it's happening. In what sense is this a "rug" or this a "knee"? It's actually an infinite, unknown, incredibly complex thing which is one with the whole causal matrix of the universe of consciousness. And what does THAT mean?!? It's more simplifications, but saying it's a rug or a knee doesn't capture the reality of that, can't capture that. You can call it a rug or a knee but it's a finger pointing at the moon. THIS isn't a knee, THIS isn't a rug. I'm designating this by the symbol "rug", this by the symbol "knee"; but what are "they" REALLY? In reality there are no knees or rugs here, and no "here" here.

-So it's just pure consciousness...

Yeah. But even that, just because you've called it consciousness, don't think that you know what THAT is. What's consciousness? It's a miracle. It's the absolute presence of the miraculous. You can say there's presence and awareness, you know, we have these words; but the reality of what that IS is a mind fuck. But at the same time it's totally obvious and totally intimate. But clearly that's all that there is. There's that and this, but in reality there's no this and that. There's just "it", and then there's not even "it".

So as soon as you're using language you're just stuck in this realm of paradox and confusion. That's a very powerful topic to reflect on because we're all subliminally conditioned by language and by symbols, on the supposition that there's some kind of one-to-one correlation between symbols and reality; that they have some veracity, that they have some degree of correspondence with the actual nature of things. And they DON'T! They're like waving your hands. The most precise language in the world boils down to like (Peter waves his hands).

-We'll be in the middle of a discussion and then we just wave our hands like monkeys.

Seeing that is seeing the true situation with language.

-The more I say I don't know, the more clear things are becoming...

Letting go of knowing is actually very empowering. We're left with the truth of being. Even in the midst of our illusion of stories, we have a certainty that we're faking it... "I've built up all this status and I'm this smart guy. I've got all these tricks I can pull out of my hat; but, in the back of my mind I know I'm faking it. In the back of my mind I know it's all bullshit. I'm just trying to impress people because I'm afraid that I'm only a stupid little boy." So, when you say "I don't know" and mean it, you're bypassing that whole neurosis. You're bypassing that whole identification with yourself as a defined entity, and resting in the openness of Being itself. It's ultimately freeing. It's empowering; and all of the posturing is ultimately unempowering because it's based on the unconsciously-known certainty that it's a lie.

And unconsciously we KNOW this, so we get more defensive and belligerent. "Yeah, but I'm real sharp! And I know this and that and blah blah blah..." But the more I push that out, the more I'm pulling on my inadequacy, the more I'm actually asserting the fact that I know I'm full of bullshit. But when you let go and say "I don't know" that whole game is disempowered, and you cut to the chase of your true being; which is enormously empowering because it's REAL. It's not based on a posturing, it's based on actuality. We DON'T actually know. If you don't know, you don't know. How can one know? What can one know? Anything that we know is a posturing, which is hollow and unempowering. It's something we define into existence ultimately, so hence, it's a lie, or at least a leap of faith or an assumption at best.

-So I know that I don't know...

You can't even know that you don't know.

The only spirituality is seeing reality, anything else is just lifestyle choices. You may as well join a different club, which is what most "spirituality" actually consists of. Go become a Buddhist, a Christian, Hari Krishna, clothing choices, behavior choices, which rituals am I going to use; should I wear my mala on my left hand or my right hand... which is just gamesmanship. It has nothing to do with seeing reality. You may as well just join a political party. Unfortunately most spirituality is just masquerading as a roadway to reality, to freedom, to God. You're being sold a bill of goods. You got on this road that supposedly is leading you to God, and all they're leading you to is their own internally referential gamesmanship. The way to God is to abandon ALL games. And you don't even need to abandon them to abandon them, just know that they're games, and stop giving a shit about them.

-Does that mean you can still participate in the game?

Of course. You CAN'T stop participating to some extent, unless you have an unusual nature. You are the expression of the energies that constitute your being. And that expression of energy has a life of its own, so to speak, and will continue to unfold in the way that it's unfolding; which COULD include radical changes, if that's in its nature to have. So all your behavior is inherent in what you ARE. You will continue to function as you, whatever that happens to end up looking like. The point about all the "gamesmanship" and all the lies is that they don't matter, they're not true, it doesn't matter what we do; none of it actually effects what we actually and inherently ARE. THAT'S where enlightenment lies, NOT in what we DO.

Reality is ALREADY AND ALWAYS doing itself. Reality is a done deal. Enlightenment is a done deal. God is the only one in this room. The only one in this universe. So after THAT, just amuse yourself. What difference does it make? You can't subtract from the perfection of Being. You can't add to it either, so what difference does it make? But on the other hand, what you're inclined to do is what you're inclined to do. YOU didn't choose that. The universe did. It's all the will of God.

-How do you remember this?

Basically, you're screwed. (laughter) You ultimately have to get lucky. You have to notice. You have to find yourself arriving through circumstances or good fortune at a place where you can see IT as it is. It seems to happen on its own eventually. It's like the proverbial muddy water that clears and eventually settles. It's a natural process of maturing. You get to a certain point in your experience and you begin to notice things. Till then, you're just like a small child. You don't notice much of anything.

It's like a quarterback sneak in football, forgetting the usual pattern of things and just going for it! You can let the game be what it is, and just poke your head outside for a minute. Eventually, you get to a point where this becomes an important thing for you, and at that point you're investment starts to be in THAT. There's less investment in the games and confusion. You gradually weary and withdraw your attention from that struggle, that ultimately futile struggle to make sense of the chaos. And you begin to invest your attention more and more in the core of your Being, in the essence of what is.

You see it when you see it. Looking for it is no guarantee you'll find it, but it's a natural process. It's not something you can contrive or try to do. After a while, we weary of the shallowness of life. We weary of the hollowness. We weary of the hopelessness of it and begin to want to look deeper. We begin to say "God, this sucks, this doesn't make any sense, this is crazy, there has got to be more". And that's when we start to look deeper, and it's that natural urge to search that brings about finding it. That and luck.

That investment in our games is the only thing blinding us, because there's actually nothing BUT the obvious fact, that things are the way they are. It's an obvious fact that things are just energies cascading through consciousness, never repeating, constantly changing. This same instant never happens twice. This is totally obvious, but we forget it. We get hypnotized in our fantasies that these are persistent "things" that stay the same (points around room), and think we're stuck in them; rather than seeing they are totally unknown mysteries, chaotically moving around like a waterfall. Which is manifestly the fact. If you look closely at your experience, it's just a whirlwind of crazy shit happening. It's really pretty obvious, when you can step back enough to see it. But when we're invested in trying to MAKE something of things, that's what blinds us to what things really are. It's like you're watching TV and some show comes on, and you start getting really invested in the characters and the plot and all that. You forget that you're just watching little flickers of light that are showing up on the TV screen. There IS no plot. There ARE no people, just flashes of light; but the seduction of the investment in those so called interesting things, draws our attention. It sucks us in, draws our attention away from being able to step away and see things as they ACTUALLY are.

It's a natural process. We eventually weary of it and begin to change our focus. It's a spiritual maturity.

It's all a matter of noticing. We NEVER really DO anything. Even when we think we're doing something, if we look close enough, there are forces welling up in consciousness which are doing the motivating. And we identify, saying "Oh I'M doing this." But if you look very closely, it's just this upwelling of energy, upwelling of motivation. Where does it come from? Where does it go to? It's a mystery. And that mystery is what we truly are.

It's a matter of noticing. If we don't notice then we get sucked in to thinking, "I'm doing this, this is important to me, I'm involved with this. This matters, this doesn't matter. I don't like this, I'm going to achieve this, I'm going to avoid this"; and all of a sudden we have this entire comic book that we're reading in our minds, that we call our life. But it's all a myth. And it won't happen exactly as we hope or fear it will, even if we succeed in approximating it; which is a very rare thing. It STILL won't happen just so, because there is nothing that's in anyone's control. Things just happen the way they do.

-Sometimes I have trouble letting go of people who lie to me and say that it's all the will of God, that they're not responsible.

Some people spend their lives lying and shitting on other people. It's a manifest truth. How can they do that? Because they're the kind of people that behave like that. Why are they the kind of people that behave like that? Because that's the way the system of the the universe made them.

-How can someone be Enlightened and still perpetrate that kind of action?

Enlightenment has NOTHING to do with action. Maybe that person was a child murderer in their last life and they've improved to the point where they're just a con man. It's a big move in the right direction. (laughter) Look at the bright side.

My brother was an alcoholic, but we thought he was doing great because he wasn't a junkie anymore. We thought how wonderful, he's an alcoholic. Big improvement. In context for HIM, he was doing great. His self loathing was way down. His functional behavior was up slightly. And for HIM that was great. You gotta put things into context.

Behavior is about being what the universe made you. Behavior is inevitable. You are what you are and you're going to do what you do. Some people are getting drunk at a bar right now. Other people are coming to Satsangs and listening to Satsang. Other people are home torturing children. Why?

-Sometimes I despair of ever really getting it...

It's a process of maturing. Just like an infant. A one month old infant can't feed itself, can't clean itself, can't do anything, and it gradually very very slowly matures to some degree of functionality. And this is all a natural unfolding in the way that things unfold. It's a natural process.

And the same with our spiritual process of maturing. It happens as it happens. It's a very long, drawn out, slow process. It happens when it happens, AS it happens. It doesn't happen just because you want it to. The child doesn't learn to tie its shoes because it wants to. He learns by doing it badly many times, and then finally getting it. Toilet training happens gradually and slowly. Finally, "Oh I get it!". But that's a revelation that comes after a lot of "whoops!". And our spiritual unfoldment is exactly the same.

The point is we're each individually where we are. And we CAN'T be other than where we are. And where THAT is, is where we ARE in this process of unfolding, and that process of unfolding is inevitable. And we have nothing to do with it anyway, so why even bother about it. It's not like we have a choice. We can't DECIDE to be less spiritually or more spiritually open than we are. You are where you are. Surrender to that process. Surrender to the divine plan, surrender to the universal consciousness, surrender to the patterns of being or whatever you want to call it. Whether you surrender or NOT, it has GOT you already; it's a done deal.

-I feel like I've always been searching... if it's luck and I'm not lucky then I'm screwed...

You never have to wait, really, because there's nothing BUT luck. Luck's happening right now. There's nothing but luck, there's nothing but chance. How did you happen to come here? How do you happen to be thinking these thoughts? It's ALL luck! It's all chance and it's all a part of the process of your unfolding, which will look the way it will look.

-Are luck and karma the same?

Exactly, different words for different models of EXACTLY the same thing, the flow of events.

It's an inevitable process, so you don't need to despair about anything. You're ALREADY it. It is inevitable that you will know that and see that since you truly want to, since you're at the point where you're feeling that. You're craving that. The process of unfoldment looks the way it looks at any particular time, WHATEVER it happens to look like. Sometimes it looks like wanting, sometimes it looks like despair, some times it looks like "Oh fuck it, I'm going to go out and party". Sometimes it looks like finding. But each stage is not lesser than any other. The stage of finding isn't any better than the stage of wanting, or any better than the stage of saying "Screw it".

They are all stages in exactly the same process, the same trajectory. To say THIS part of the trajectory is better than

THAT part of the trajectory is foolish. It just looks like this now, then this now, and this now. (moves hand along an arc) But it's the one trajectory. It may be hard to know that or have faith in that, depending on which part of the trajectory you're in, but it's still the truth.

It only APPEARS to take time. There's no such thing as time actually. Time is the essence of the mystery. Look at what time is and you'll have the solution to everything; because if you see where time is, you'll see where reality is. It's an infinite mystery. Time is an infinite mystery, space is an infinite mystery, being itself is an infinite mystery. Identity is an infinite mystery. Functioning is, energy is...

You need to say, "Hey wait a minute. Lets just assume that I don't know anything. And lets assume that my maps are completely wrong. Where does that leave me?" Look and see. Don't THINK about it. Just look and see. "If I don't know what I am, if I don't know where I am, if I don't have a clue what's happening right now; where am I?" LOOK and SEE what that is. It's very obvious. But we have to drop the usual investment in all this complexity, to just let go and say, "Well, I don't know". Start from I don't know and stay there, and see what that IS. What does "I don't know" look like? It looks like all this. (waves hand to indicate space)

We're hypnotized. We don't know we're doing a map, we think we're doing an actuality.

We don't need to FIX our personality to be free of our personality. We just need to see what it is. We don't need to fix or stop our ego to be free of our ego. We just need to see what it is. All those things are just modes of energy, and we just need to see the truth of that. It's like a TV that's on in the corner of the room. We don't have to pay attention to it. We don't even need to turn it off. We just need to see that it's just a TV.

But it's OURSELVES that we're slicing up conceptually by thinking we're one thing or another, so of course we're crazy. It's our state to be in that position at certain points of our evolution. It's not a BAD thing. It's just what it looks like. It's like a chicken in an eggshell. The chick being in the eggshell is not a bad thing, and the chick's breaking out of the eggshell is not a good thing; they just LOOK different, they're just different phases of the same process. Likewise, at different times in our evolution we look really confused, and at other times we look much less confused. But the one isn't necessarily BETTER than the other, just different portions of our trajectory. It's like now the flower is closed, then now the flower is open. It looks very DIFFERENT, but it's not better or worse. It's just different phases of development of the same thing. It's all a process and it has the same trajectory, the same value whether it's in the beginning or the middle or the end of the trajectory, because it's just the one thing. So whatever phase you're in, you're at the goal. The goal just happens to look like it looks at this particular moment. One day the moment might look more like what you would think of as being the goal. It's all exactly the same goal, this is just what it looks like right now. A rose is a rose when it's a petal or a seed, it's just in a different phase of its unfoldment.

The whole thing with maps is an art, and it's tricks. You're tricking yourself. Just because it's a map doesn't mean it's bad. Just because it's a map doesn't mean it can't work. It's just not the whole truth; but it can still be useful. Maps can get us to the grocery store. But there IS no grocery store and there are no groceries. THAT'S the truth, but the maps still get us to the grocery store. It's a koan.

So again, it's a matter of not being trapped by maps, not a matter of not HAVING maps. The more artfully you play with it and explore it, and the more you learn those differentiations, the more you can navigate and let yourself surf your experience. Surfing is a good analogy. Surf your own energy. Get to know your own energy. That's what Tantra is. Learn all the energies in your reality. They're all you. Own them. Go with them, travel them.

It's all a matter of acquiring perspective. NOTHING needs to be different than it is. You just need to see what it ACTUALLY is from the broadest possible perspective. Navigating our energy is a process of exploring perspectives. What does my reality look like from this perspective... what does my reality look like from THIS perspective. And if you do that with enough abandon and enough depth of experience, you ultimately can stumble on the TRUE perspective of what we really are. From the point of view of what we really are, everything clicks. Everything falls into place, clarity is there.

A perfect analogy is the wonderful computer generated puzzles that look like squiggles. If you look at them for a while, all of a sudden they resolve themselves into a 3d image. The difference between seeing it and not seeing it is the trick of finding the right perspective. That's how it is in finding the truth of spiritual perspective in reality. And the only thing that keeps us from doing that is: we're locked into our habitual perspective and we think that's IT, and we don't ever bother to look around. Let your perspective be free. Get drunk every now and then. Take drugs, meditate. Do different things. Let yourself navigate your experience in new ways, and see the different pieces of it. Push the boundaries. Sensually. Don't think about it, BE it. See what it feels like, drink it in with its texture. And as you do that, you're actually seeing the universe in different perspectives. You may stumble on a perspective that opens into the perspective of Being itself...

You don't need to change anything, you just need to see what it IS in its true perspective, because it's ALL just energy in consciousness. It's self-originating. You don't need anything to be different. You can go into a wild party, you can go into a rock club, you can go to a beautiful stream in the middle of the woods, and it's all ultimately exactly the same. You appreciate the differences, but you don't need one to be the other; because it's ALL just energy in consciousness.

The bottom line is that we need to trust the process, trust being itself. Being is already BEING being, so who are WE to second guess it? Trust the process that is already going on. The process is us, we ARE that process, it's already happening; so, what's the problem? And having it LOOK like a problem is itself in THAT instant the process. It IS us. It is what we are. It's what we're being in that period of time.

Again, we just have to trust the process, open to our being. Open to the reality of our experience. Trust our experience, trust our experience itself. Seeing what we're seeing, hearing what we're hearing, thinking what we're thinking, feeling what we're feeling, because THAT is opening to reality. That in itself is opening up to God; because God IS the reality that is happening right now right here. Pure and simple. There's no smoke or mirrors.

And we're ALREADY that, we just need to notice it. We don't really NEED to notice it, but sooner or later we will; consciousness will always ultimately know itself.

-What's the difference between being spaced out and being enlightened?

No difference. They are in essence one and the same. Ultimately spacing out IS enlightenment. It's relaxing the fixation. It's letting go of identity. It's letting go of "I am this, I am not that". That's what samadhi means. It's letting go of your mind. Spacing out is letting go of everything. Let things go their way. Enlightenment is seeing that there is absolutely nothing you can do or not do, or need to do. So at that point, ABSOLUTELY nothing matters. It's a totally done deal. And it's ALL there.

It's freedom from importance. Importance is a really good measure of our liberation, because importance is always SELF importance. Self importance is investment in the ego. Anything in phenomena that feels important: the war's important, the presidency is important, watching someone else fail is important, enlightenment is important; is an indication of our investment in ego, and our imaginary sense of self. The true index of enlightenment is when NOTHING is important to us. YOU don't have importance, they don't have importance. Everything is even, equal, a level playing field and it's playing itself. So, what does that leave? It leaves ANYTHING. It leaves everything. But

LEAVE is the operative word; there's nothing whatever that needs doing. And if it DOES need doing, it gets done "by itself".

Looking for fulfillment... What fulfillment actually is, is reality itself; reality is nothing BUT fulfillment. It's fullness, it's completeness, it's nourishment, it's release. In Tibetan they call it Dzogchen, which means "great completion", great perfection. Because it's a sea of fullness... and you know, how yummy is that?

Anytime we find a partial satisfaction in an experience, we're just seeing a small aspect or echo of THAT; but THAT is actually our very nature, and the inherent nature of experience itself. We have it, ARE it, all the time. It's the very nature of every object, of every subject, the very nature of the fact that we're experiencing.

But by NOT seeing that we deprive ourselves of it, and we think that we feel emptiness and that we need to look somewhere for something to fill us up, to ring our bell, to complete us.

-...You mean the usual way we see things?

Yes. Our habitual ways of looking at things are our enemy. Not our enemy in the sense that we need to stop them, they're our enemy in the sense that we need to see what they REALLY are, so we can see around them and not have our true experience obscured by them.

It's like a play; if you're in a theater, and there's a play onstage and you're getting all involved in Shakespeare and

Hamlet's about to kill himself and so on, there's also an infinite amount of other stuff going on. There's the theater, there're the people next to you, there's the feeling of the seat on your butt and the temperature of the air, and your subliminal thoughts and moods, the sensations of your skin and body; there's all this other stuff too. But we're generally not noticing all that, we're locked into the play. So we don't need to stop the play from happening or enjoying it, we just need to notice that it's a play, and be aware of our complete reality. Notice that we're in a theater watching a play; notice the full context, the full content of our actual experience.

The way to do that is by LOOKING. Look and see. And if you come up against a really "sticky" belief, where you feel "No! It's GOTTA be like this!", then look more carefully, use your analysis, use your discriminating intelligence. Ask yourself "Is this really true? Can I KNOW for certain that this is actually true?"; and if not, discard it as being a certainty, it's useless, it's trash. The bottom line is that ANY belief whatsoever cannot be true, simply because reality is ultimately a mystery, and it CANNOT be accurately described in human language as it is.

NO ONE'S GOING TO DO IT FOR US. WE have to look, AND SEE, for ourselves. Everyone's trying to tell you, "THIS is how it is"; I am too. You go to the Pope, he'll tell you "THIS is how it is". You go to the Dalai Lama, he'll tell you "THIS is how it is". You can get a million and one interpretations describing "this is how reality IS"; but YOU'RE the one who ultimately has to decide for yourself what's true, and the only way to do that is to get off your butt and SEE how it IS for yourself in realtime. All anyone else's descriptions can do is hide reality, obscure it, confuse it. Because the true nature of reality is naked and obvious to direct experience, but unfortunately indescribable in human language accurately.

-What is it?

It's up to YOU to find out! What IS it? Figure it out! "Let ME figure this out". You know? Because maybe they're wrong, you know? All these authorities with their contradictory stories can't all be right, can they? There're some pretty wild contradictions out there.

-Why CAN'T they all be right?

Well, maybe so, actually there's a way it IS so, but YOU'RE the one who has to see that, to decide that, for yourself. That's the point. The point is that the buck stops with YOU. YOU'RE the authority of your life. YOU have to find the truth. And if you settle for someone else's, then you're living THEIR truth , you know, and then who's living yours?

-So what about the enlightened guy who got up to get a beer because he was bored?

That's fine, you get up, and go get your beer; but there's no interpretation of boredom, because you know that it's ALL the ultimate flow of your reality. And even if there WAS still a feeling of boredom, THAT'S the flow, too. Within the context of the complete fullness of infinite presence, boredom is appearing, beer is appearing, getting up is appearing. But there's no problem, no issue, no strategy leading to something else, leading to some imaginary cornucopia in the sky.

-How did that first happen for you?

Well, it's a process. Our whole life is leading to our balloon popping, that's what life IS. Life IS the spiritual path.

-If we're lucky-

Yeah, it may not lead to it in the sense that you ARRIVE at it, but it's pushing you toward it, towards seeing. The very point of suffering is to motivate exploration, to motivate searching. But you're right, it takes luck, we might not "get there". It's like a plant's seeds that fall on the sidewalk; the one that falls on the concrete is at a dead end, but the one that falls in the cracks has a chance, if other conditions line up.

But the mechanism is there to motivate consciousness to search for, and ultimately find, itself.

-That's all that it does...

Yes. Simply put, the universe consists of God forgetting itself and God finding itself. We're talking about the forgetting and finding aspects with an emphasis on the finding because that's the focus of this kind of a talk, but consciousness losing itself is part of the process too; we could be easily talking about how to better lose ourselves in ignorance, that's the other side of the same coin, of the same process. (Laughter) But society's already doing that for us, this is equal time. The loyal opposition getting equal time. We got the floor, goddammit! (laughter)

-We live within a context of partiality and lies as kids, and all our lives; but some of us seem to chafe against that, and try to struggle our way out of all that.

The process of struggling against that lie, IS a process. If we're very very lucky, perhaps we can see truth, and we see through the lie instantly. But I don't think that happens very often, if at all. I think more typically we have either a subtle intuition or a more obvious integration or knowledge that looks like, "Wait a minute! Something's going on here, and I want to find out what it really is." And THAT is the spark that gets fanned into the actual search, and the struggle and the battle for cutting through the crap. Like, "Hey! I am spinning this bullshit that's pulling me into this absurdly small life that I think I'm living, and where's the satisfaction? Where's the richness? And if it's based on lies, if it's a lie, I don't want it anymore. I say NO. So what do I do now?"

And the answer to that is, ANYTHING YOU CAN. That's the answer to that, anything you can. Analyze. Struggle. Think about it. Meditate. Feel. Open all avenues of exploration. It's like if you want to break out of jail, how do you do it? You try EVERYTHING. You try bribing the guards, you try digging, you try and find a loose bar. Try everything! If it really matters to you, you've gotta DO it! YOU'VE got to make it happen; anyway you can.

-You always say that social success is a trap, and failure is our biggest teacher...

Failure is wonderful. It's a blessing to fail, because it motivates you to investigate what the fuck is going on. But if you have worldly success, you'll think "All right! I won the game! Let's do it some more and win some more..." It pulls us deeper and deeper into getting stuck in this imaginary social game structure, blinding us to our actual nature.

-So spiritual seekers are all misfits-

Sure, pretty much by definition. If you're really successful in life, what's the motivation to rock the boat? You know? It's like, "Hey! This is working big time for me, I'm a movie star, making lots of money, everyone loves me, I have great sex, fast cars, this that and the other... I'm on top of the world! Why should I investigate or question anything?" Except maybe as an adjunct to my ego, "Hey, I'm really spiritual, too."

-I read a book that describes enlightenment as "disappointment"...

Yes. The process can be, anyway. Seeing reality brings the loss of everything we've ever held dear in the old way we've valued it. It's seeing that all our most precious stories about ourselves are hollow. It's seeing that the life we thought we were living is all worthless. And there's not even anyone to care about that loss, or to enjoy that stuff if it WAS true. Because in reality there's no one there, there's no thing there, so it's a total loss in terms of what was hoped for, what was expected. I've been painting it from the point of view that it's ecstasy, but it's also absolutely nothing, emptiness, absolute void. It's truly the death of the individual, that which we've always feared, because it's the loss of ALL separation, the loss of all individuality, the loss of self. BUT, it's not really a loss either, because nothing is lost. Everything is just seen for what it is and has always been. There never WAS any substance to these pretty sentiments that we valued so much, they were NEVER real. And we've always kind of known that, which is why we struggle so much to validate them and glorify them. If they were real, we could just sit back and let them take care of themselves; but we've always kind of known that we were pretending, wishfully thinking "I really WANT this to be true".

-So disappointment, ecstasy, pretending, are all qualities of reality...

EVERY quality is reality. They're just some of the ways reality can appear to be. The way reality actually IS is WAY beyond any partial, describable aspect of how it can appear; reality is absolutely infinite, indefinable and indescribable. BUT it is readily experienceable as it is; and actually we've never done anything else.

-So everything is success, it's just kind of a watching in consciousness...

It's God watching God, as different modes of its inherent energy. EVERYTHING is just different modes of energy. The energy is the same energy, that energy just has infinite modes, and all THIS appears (waves hands). It can manifest in ANY way. But it's not worse for manifesting in one way, and better in another.

-Would an enlightened being with Alzheimer's be affected by it?

There's no "them" to be affected. Being "enlightened" means the perceiver is known with certainty to be beyond circumstances, outside the dream. You KNOW you're the dreamer of this dream, now, and that "you're" not in it. If you DON'T know that, you think you're in the dream; if you DO know that, then you're the dreamer, free of the circumstances appearing in the dream. An "enlightened" person knows they're not IN the experience that they're having, so it doesn't matter what the experience IS.

Anyway, this kind of speculation is pointless. The point is, what's going on right here right now with YOU. Are YOU enlightened? Are you IN the dream? Are you the dreamer? Look at THAT, see what's going on with that.

-Sometimes I see that it's like a dream, but sometimes I have doubts...

Keep looking at what's your relationship to it, to being. Are you IN it, ARE you it, what? Are you in being, or are you being itself? And if you think you're IN being, and not being itself, what are you made of? How did you come to be that? Where does it come from? In what is it existing?

-So I think I'm in the dream, and something bad could happen to me or something...

The crux of that is what you mean by "me". If you think "me" is that body there, that personality complex that acts in certain ways and other people react to, and so on, then all of a sudden you're vulnerable. But if you're the consciousness beyond space and time that's EXPERIENCING all this (and I suggest if you look you'll see that you manifestly ARE that), in what way can what happens to your character in this experience affect THAT?

When you get sick does your consciousness get sick? When you succeed does your consciousness succeed? When you fail, does your consciousness fail? It is always PERFECTLY clear and present, unmediatedly knowing these apparent circumstances. "Alex" is just a character in a drama. The consciousness that's experiencing that, is always completely clear, completely present; and when you say "me", what meaningfully can you be referring to other than IT? Look and see, look and see for yourself.

-It's like you're trying to tell us that the Earth is not round...

I'm saying there's no Earth.

-But then there's a benevolent freedom when you do see it...

It's TOTALLY benevolent. Because then you see that you're FREE of all this stuff that you thought was so important. You see that (A) IT is doing itself entirely, it doesn't need any effort from us that it doesn't supply itself, and (B) it's already all YOU, it's what you actually ARE and have always been. You're not separate from it, so there's no danger, no personal precariousness. You're like a fish made of water in the middle of the ocean. What could be safer or more complete? And IT'S the unstoppable fountain of all this experience, all this entertainment...

-But we've all been so stuck in our belief systems, we all believe that the earth is round. But that's just a belief, we can't really say...

Exactly. But that's hard to demonstrate to a person that's hypnotized into that belief. All I'm really saying is doubt your beliefs. And if you do that successfully and free yourself from them as assumed certainties, what that leaves you with is the immediacy of your actual experience, and the certainty that any interpretations you put on it are arbitrary.

-Right. Because when you release that belief, you fall into the only thing that's real anyway, what remains after the beliefs have gone.

Yeah. When you stop believing anything, what's left? What's there that doesn't go away? THAT'S reality. Reality is what's there whether or not you're believing in it, you can't make it go away through changing belief or stopping belief. The certainty of a "round Earth" falls away pretty fast if you investigate, but the fact of experiencing DOESN'T.

But to describe experience AT ALL just suggests more belief systems. In truth, we can't say WHAT it is! Even when I say it's "energy in consciousness", that implies a belief system. But that's a way of pointing to a simpler, less inaccurate belief system than the complex mazes we usually inhabit, which involve worlds in solar systems and billions of beings, with politics, war, poisoning the environment, "Oh my God, we're all going to die"; THAT'S a complex belief. If you can collapse all that down to "Oh, there's energy in consciousness", that's a major step in the right direction, although not the final stop.

Then let go of "energy in consciousness"; and WHERE are you? You can't even say "here". Can't even say "now". But it is what we ARE, whatever it is. And what we've ALWAYS been, even when we were in the midst of all that hardcore believing. Look at it. SEE it.

-Do you kind of get that, then lose it, then get it again, until it settles in...

NO. What happens is you get an APPROXIMATION of it then lose THAT, then get another approximation, and so on. It's when you give up on approximations that you finally see, dumbfounded, that "Oh my god, I've been IT all along, and I even KNEW it! But I was so caught up and it was so simple I just couldn't believe it." You CAN'T ever lose it because you were never anything but. There has never BEEN anything else. But, we don't appreciate it.

In old alchemical texts from the middle ages, they say "you take the most common, worthless thing that everyone discards", and THAT'S what you make the philosopher's stone from. And that's exactly analogous to this. The one thing that people completely devalue and think nothing of is the fact of being. We love what we own, what we want, what we make, what we cling to, even what we avoid; but ALL that is happening WITHIN being, and being is always there, it's the constant.

And the fact is that being is ENORMOUSLY powerful. It's even beyond powerful; it's EVERYTHING. It's God: it's the presence of the divine. It's doing all this, and it IS all this, and all this boils down to nothing but that. But we don't acknowledge the amazing way that being IS us and all this, we don't appreciate it. And when you SEE that, you can't lose it or find it or anything, because you and everything ARE it; there's nothing to find and nothing to loose. It's so obvious, how can we miss it? We don't value what's indescribably valuable, what's indescribably precious. We undervalue it and we think that there's something ELSE that's valuable, our pet obsessions, and we go chasing rainbows to try and find the pot of gold at the end of them. But the pot of gold has been right here, right now, always.

But what's DOING the chasing, is it itself. It does everything. And what succeeds or fails in our endeavors is it itself. But we don't see that until we see it. To arrive at the spiritual maturity in our unfoldment where we start trying to look for it in the right place, where IT IS, happens when it happens.

The reality of our experience can look like being a yogi in the Himalayas, or can look like sitting in front of the TV drinking a beer and watching Seinfeld reruns. But in reality there's ABSOLUTELY no difference between the two. That's the secret, and that's what we don't see, the seeing of which is the final gate of spirituality. We get caught up by the glamour of appearances, "this is better than that".

Consciousness is so miraculous, and so obvious and intimate. But we're so busy looking OUT of it we rarely look AT it. It CAN see itself; consciousness can see itself. Consciousness can see what it is, can plumb its own depths. In fact it never does anything else, all our experience is nothing else; but when we realize that and become active participants in that, we have entered spiritual maturity.

-The preconceptions of mainstream science preclude so many "spiritual" phenomena making sense; but if we look from the point of view of consciousness being the fundamental basis, then so much parapsychology and spiritual phenomena can begin to make sense. Like looking back at our bodies in a hospital...

We're constantly looking back at our bodies. (laughter). Where are we looking at our bodies from? THAT'S the mystery. Consciousness is infinitely mobile. Consciousness doesn't have location; locations occur IN consciousness.

-A friend of mine was joking about going to "Satsangs anonymous"... I wonder; when you get the message, don't you hang up the phone?

Yeah.

-But it seems that there's an unending opening up...

Yes. It's unending opening by its very nature. But you DO arrive at certainty, that you hadn't had previously: then finally you see the truth directly (which has been described as "it's all mind" or "God does everything" or "I'm one with the universe" or "I am not my body", and in so many other ways), and that certainty stays with you. You know you ARE it, and have always been it. And with that certainty you lose all need for anything more. There IS an end of the searching, but no end to the opening.

Made in the USA
Las Vegas, NV
30 June 2021